Know

Gvirtz

Don't Say we didn't Know
Amos Gvirtz

Editor: Maxine Kaufman-Lacusta
Translated from the Hebrew by Tal Haran

Contact: amosg@shefayim.org.il
ISBN 9781790791552

DON'T SAY WE DIDN'T KNOW

AMOS GVIRTZ

Contents

INTRODUCTION

A few years ago, Ya'acov Manor and I went to the Intensive Care Unit of Beilinson Hospital to visit an elderly Palestinian man who had been beaten unconscious by settlers from Elon Moreh. We sat talking with the injured man's son. Another Palestinian, there to visit his sick brother, joined our conversation. He told us how he had suffered at the hands of teenage boys from the Israeli settlement beside his village, which repeatedly broke through the fence around his cistern and urinated into it.

At that moment I thought to myself, there are thousands of such stories that don't get told and that none of us Israelis hear about. They are part of the ongoing chronicle of the occupation. This realization led me to undertake the project that I call "Don't Say We Did Not Know." I was born in 1946, only a year after the hostilities of World War II in Europe ended. Stories of the Holocaust were a part of my world growing up, and I assume that they were a part of the world of every Jew of our generation. We were told that many Germans claimed that they had been unaware of the genocide being carried out by the Nazis. We always said that they didn't want to know.

In 1976, as I recall, I found out about the genocide being committed by the Khmer Rouge following their takeover of Cambodia. Naively, I prevailed upon some Israeli Communists to speak out against that genocide. I assumed that there was a greater chance of the Khmer Rouge regime being influenced by fellow Communists' condemnation of that appalling slaughter than by that of those who were known to be committed opponents of the regime. To my astonishment, I was met with flat refusal to acknowledge that what was going on was genocide. Most of the people I appealed to claimed there was no genocide and that this was capitalist propaganda aimed at discrediting the Cambodian revolution (only when Cambodia became party to the USSR-China conflict, did Communists begin to speak of the genocide that had taken place there…). The only one who admitted to me at the time that genocide was taking place said that he would not speak against the revolution. At the same time, I witnessed how Israelis refuse to acknowledge the crimes that Israel has committed against its own Palestinian minority as well as against Palestinians in the Occupied Territories. I saw how the Turks refuse to acknowledge the genocide that they committed against the Armenians during World War I.

I realized that this was a universal phenomenon - members of an "identity group" (such as a national or ethnic group) refusing to "know" and to acknowledge crimes perpetrated by their own group. So I decided on the name, "Don't Say We Did Not Know" for this project. Of course, the question remained, what was the point of undertaking such a project, given the extremely important work being done by *B'tselem* (The Israeli Information Center for Human Rights in The Occupied Territories)? Why take this on when journalists like Gideon Levy and Amira Hass of *Ha'aretz* were doing such a good job?

Sadly, no such work is being done regarding the Negev Bedouins. The only body whose work in this area resembles that of *B'tselem* is the Negev Coexistence Forum for Civil Equality. Not one Jewish journalist is reporting on the house demolitions, destruction of villages and crops, and restrictions on grazing imposed upon the Bedouin in the Negev by the Israeli authorities in an effort to force them to abandon their villages and what little land remains to them and move into the "planned towns." This is the reason I make such a point of reporting on house demolitions and crop destruction in the Negev.

It's important to recall that as this book was being written, there were only 240,000 Bedouin in the Negev. Even so, the government of Israel demolishes far more homes there annually than it dares to in the West Bank - and with scarcely any coverage by the Hebrew media. When one knows nothing of the history of relations between successive Israeli governments and the Negev Bedouins, the government's claims against them might appear justified. Familiarity with this history and with what is currently happening in the Negev makes it clear that the Bedouins are in the right. In fact, when reports do appear in the Hebrew media, they usually take the government's side against the Bedouins without providing any background information

I would not presume to put myself in the same class as *B'tselem* or Amira Haas or Gideon Levy. I am neither a researcher nor a journalist. I see myself as an activist for peace and human rights who for many years has focused on bringing a perspective of nonviolence to our conflict, and on stopping the process of expelling the Palestinians from this country – a process that in my view is at the heart of the conflict. Until recently, my activism was limited to the end of my workday and weekends, so I had neither the time nor ability to accomplish anything with the depth of their excellent work.

In our modern age, we are all inundated with tremendous amounts of information coming at us from every direction. Thus, I thought, there would be a greater chance that people would have sufficient time and patience to read about the terrible events I report on if I wrote very summarily about these incidents. Tales of human rights violations do not usually interest the average reader who isn't their victim. The idea, then, is that this brevity would encourage people to take the trouble to read, and they would not get bored before finishing. As a proponent of nonviolence, I regard the "public eye" as a significant nonviolent weapon.

There are four "traditional" ways to examine the Israeli-Palestinian conflict: through academic research; from the standpoint of political ideology; via journalism; and the fourth, which I have chosen to follow - from the perspective of an activist in the field, routinely exposed to local realities - by means of which I attempt to grasp the underlying state policies.

I regard myself essentially as a peace and human rights activist and the blog, "Don't Say We Did Not Know," as an important part of my activism. Most of the cases I describe are taken from reports by Israeli and international human rights organizations, including the UN agency OCHA, or from direct reports by other activists. I find utmost importance in always verifying the information I receive via telephone. I have often refrained from reporting a case because I found no source who could verify what I had read and expand upon my knowledge of the incident - however much I wished to report it. Even so, I am certain there are occasional slipups. I recall several cases where I was made aware of this and reported my error. I do not know how many times I have erred and not been corrected. No one is infallible, certainly not I.

I wish that these incidents had never taken place… And it's important to note that I have never turned to the spokespersons of the army or the settlers for information. The Hebrew media are replete with their narrative; and for me it's important to convey a different narrative, one to which Israelis are hardly ever exposed.

The book you hold in your hands is an attempt to present the conflict from a moral standpoint which, I believe, to a great extent directs my activism and how I relate to events. In this book I try to understand why we peace and human rights activists arouse so much anger and opposition. After all, most of those whom we anger so much claim to want peace, too. I offer some thoughts about the important role of the peace and human rights movement in ending or preventing genocidal wars. Perhaps this is our greatest success, of which we are entirely unaware! I try to understand why the peace movement is so small and ineffectual most of the time. Perhaps the question is not why we fail but how we ever managed to succeed the few times we did. Based on this analysis, I attempt to propose how I think we should act in order to have even the slightest chance of success. I propose the path of nonviolence and the vision/theory of "an escalation of nonviolence." I offer my understanding of the nature of the conflict and the implications of such understanding. For example, how does one perceive the very concept "war"? In my opinion, Israelis' understanding of this concept is very different from how Palestinians see it. If we do not understand the differences in this regard, then our understanding of the conflict itself is highly problematic. I offer my knowledge of how the law is used as a tool for gaining control of the land, and the consequences of such use: the clash between law and morality.

A chapter which I found personally difficult was the one on the ethical question. I believe I reached a surprising conclusion from an ethical point of view.

I attempt to understand why Israel acts the way it does, and the nature of what appear to be the two main streams in today's Zionism: the existential and the zealot-like. I think that - not unlike in the days of the destruction of the Second Temple – once more the zealot faction is jeopardizing our very existence.

In the 1980s I traveled quite extensively in Europe. I was not a typical tourist. I was seeking out pacifists, communes, and peace movements. This was a time when the anti-nuclear movement in Europe was gaining strength in its struggle against the positioning of nuclear missiles such as the Cruise and Pershing 2 there. I recall one of the slogans that touched me deeply: "Think globally; act locally."

I am an activist, not a scientist, journalist, or politician. So this book is largely informed by my many years of experience in the field. This kind of activity leads one to see things much differently than do other perspectives. Thus I reached my own insights regarding the Israeli-Palestinian conflict in particular and the Israeli-Arab conflict in general. Some of these were alarming even to me, and I am quite apprehensive about sharing them. Did our leaders really intend to achieve peace when they signed the Oslo Accords? Have the governments of Israel ever really wanted peace? Is Israel jeopardizing its own existence, as did the Apartheid regime in South Africa? That regime was replaced and the whites remained. The difference between the two conflicts causes me to question whether we will be able to survive here in the long term.

I assume there will be many who, if they take the trouble to read the book, will be angered. "What?!" they ask, "Do you actually deny our right to be here?"

We may have that right, but we don't have the right to expel those who were here before. We have the power to do so, but when we do, I fear that, sadly, we negate our right to live here. What a pity!

I intended this book as one continuous sequence of events. There were several points that I wanted to expand upon, but did not wish to interrupt the flow, so I expounded on them in accompanying essays. I believe that some of my most important statements are contained in those essays.

INTRODUCTION TO THE ENGLISH EDITION

Following the publication of this book in Hebrew I underwent a period where I was feeling somewhat empty. I felt that I had said everything I had to say and had nothing new to contribute to the discussion. To my joy, it didn't take long before new ideas began cropping up. During the process of the English editing, I made a number of revisions to the Hebrew text: I added a chapter on the "The left's unaware inner split"; I rewrote the chapter " The Difficulties Facing the Peace Movement and the Human Rights Movement"; I made some changes in the article "The ethical problem"; and finally, I added a new article " How criminalization of the victim is done".

In the Hebrew edition, examples of my short weekly reports "Don't Say We Didn't Know" were inserted between the chapters. Many readers felt that this disturbed the continuity of the reading. I have here, therefore, placed the examples at the end of the book.

I would like to express my deep gratitude to Tal Haran who translated the book into English, and to Maxine Kaufman-Lacusta who edited the English edition and adapted it for the American reader. Maxine also furnished additional context in those places where she felt that what was known to the Israeli reader might not necessarily be known to a reader who did not live the conflict directly.

PART 1

WHY PEOPLE DON'T WANT TO KNOW

LISTENING TO BOTH SIDES

It is commonly accepted that in order to deal fairly with a controversial issue, both parties must be heard. Each side sees the issue from a different perspective and relates to it accordingly. This is, after all, a fundamental principle of the legal system: For there to be any chance of a fair verdict, the judge must listen to the arguments of both sides in the controversy. Conversely, though, when it comes to a conflict between our own nation state and its adversaries, especially one that progresses to a state of war, we are expected to show absolute loyalty to our side and to ignore the requirements of morality and justice as regards the enemy.

When I take a close look at the message that I have tried to convey over my years of involvement in struggles for peace and human rights, I realize that I have consistently endeavored to inform my compatriots of the other side's narrative of the conflict, as I understand it. After all, resolving a controversy requires us to be familiar with both sides' points of view, since a peaceful outcome necessitates compromise between the opposing narratives.

FREEDOM OF CHOICE IN A PREORDAINED REALITY

You see them raiding fields not their own, incited by their rabbis in the name of "the Promise," chasing Palestinian farmers off their land and taking it over. You hear of nightly rampages through Palestinian villages, wreaking havoc on people's belongings and setting fire to mosques and to homes while their occupants sleep. You see and hear about recruitment drives following Palestinian terrorist attacks, in an attempt to enlist more support by exploiting the widespread rage and longing for vengeance. You see the hate-filled responses to news items and articles by leftist writers. If you dare to demonstrate for peace in wartime, they come after you physically. You hear their articulate spokespersons, some of whom are elected Knesset members and government ministers. And you don't know which to fear more, enemy attacks or these "patriots".

I cannot help wondering what would happen if all of these extremists were on the other side of the conflict. How we would suffer from their attacks and rhetoric! But this doesn't take much imagination. After all, that side of the conflict that our country is embroiled in has its extremists, too. Except that their being on the weaker side requires a different approach. They have no army, for example, by means of which - in an officially sanctioned manner - to express their hatred and desire to harm Israelis. Consequently some of them turn to terrorism. There, too, religious "wise men" incite believers - in this case, to go out and attack Israelis and Jews just because of who they are.

In fact, extremists are present in every ethnic group, every religion, and many an ideology. All nations have them. In Western Christian countries, we call them fascists or neo-Nazis, and they act out their hatred of those regarded as "other" as circumstances allow.

As a young man, I was tormented for years by the question of how I would have behaved had I been a German during the terrible, never-ending political crisis that swept that country in the wake of the First World War - the economy devastated and poverty rampant. Then the Nazis arrived on the scene, dramatically lowering unemployment and improving the economic situation. They brought political stability to Germany. True, they established concentration camps to which they sent political rivals, the mentally ill, and others. They attacked and incited against Jews and other minorities. And whoever dared to resist did so at their peril. It took great courage to oppose the Nazis. Of course, they labeled their opponents traitors (sound familiar?) and persecuted them. Hands on our hearts, how many of us can whole-heartedly say we are sure that we would have acted differently from most Germans at the time? How many of us would really have endangered ourselves by opposing the regime?

I came to the conclusion that only if I could place morality and justice before all other considerations, and not allow my national or other loyalties to obscure my moral judgment, would I perhaps be able to give an affirmative answer to this tormenting question.

"WE'RE THE GOOD ONES!"

Based on my experience in countless debates and struggles for peace and human rights, I would characterize most people's moral stance - in the context of conflicts between states, ethnic groups, or other "identity groups" - as "We're the good guys." This seems to be a universal phenomenon, definitely not unique to Israelis.

I've run into this any number of times in arguments and in struggles for peace and human rights. We - any "we": namely, the group we identify with - are always in the right, no matter what we do. It is always the other side that's in the wrong. We are well aware of all the harm the other side, and others have done to us, but we refuse to acknowledge the harm we do to the "other" who is not a part of our group. There is disconnection from knowledge of the harm we inflict on enemies or on others perceived as a threat. Time and again, I witness this refusal to know. And if one does know, there are always excuses to justify the harm we do, which we would never accept being done to us. There is always the "security" pretext or a legal one. Of course, it would never occur to us that we pose a threat to the other's security and often jeopardize it. We alone need security, and this is threatened or affected by the "other". When those whom we have harmed dare to defend themselves or seek revenge for what we've done to them, we're shocked: Why do these evil people attack us for no reason? We can view this through the lens of morality: We demand and try to apply moral standards amongst ourselves. However, when it comes to our treatment of another "identity group", especially one with which we are in conflict, we suddenly find all the justifications in the world for not having to adhere to those very same values.

We are unwilling to tolerate robbery, theft, property damage, violence, killing and murder, rape, etc. when they are inflicted upon members of our own group. After all, they contradict our moral values, and there are laws against such actions. But we have an army whose mandate is to do these very same things to those we regard as enemies. So when such deeds are perpetrated against those who do not belong to our "identity group" (our ethnic group, our religion, our workplace, our family, etc.), and especially against our enemies or those whom we see as a threat, they are justified on security or legal or other grounds. We are suddenly struck with moral blindness. In extreme cases, we even rejoice when we've done to our enemies the kinds of things we would never accept being done within our own society, such as killing, theft of land, violent attacks, etc. Hate and the desire for vengeance are at work here, lending legitimacy to these crimes.

EXCHANGING IDENTITIES AS A MORAL LITMUS TEST

The most important things in life are not a matter of choice, after all. We did not choose to be born; it was imposed upon us. We did not choose our birth parents; they, too, were imposed upon us. We did not choose into which nation or religion (or non-religion) to be born nor the period in which we were born. These were imposed upon us. We did not choose the upbringing we received or the values we were taught; those, too, were imposed upon us. Thus, it's obvious that fundamental aspects of our lives have been determined for us without our having had any say in the matter.

The question is what each of us does with and in the context of those predetermined factors. After all, just as I was born into a very specific reality as a Jew in Israel, I could just as well have been born an Arab, a German, an Englishman, etc. The identity of whatever group I might have been born into would have affected my values, my views, and how I related to members of groups outside my own.

Every one of the extreme nationalists I referred to earlier, had s/he been born an Arab, would have fought for Arab justice, and against Zionist crimes. They would have easily found all the arguments they needed to explain why the Zionists are criminals who must be fought to the bitter end. They would, of course, have been unaware of the crimes that their own side had committed against its enemies; or had they known about them, they would have found all the necessary justifications for those crimes. One need only recall the justifications that their religious leaders found for the all-out war they planned to wage against the Zionist Jews. After all, they had to defend their country, their farmland, their homes and lives against the Zionist invader/occupier.

All of this makes me think that the moral test here is this: If you were to change sides in the conflict, would you be able to justify the positions you had espoused and the actions you had taken before that?

The play "*They*", performed by a Jewish-Arab theater group in the 1980s, provides an excellent, concrete example of this. It tells of two women who had been born in the same hospital, on the same date in 1948: The Jew, a settler in the occupied territories, delivers a very nationalistic monologue. The Palestinian-Arab, living in a refugee camp, gives her own very nationalistic speech. They are later notified that a nurse in the hospital of their birth had accidentally switched them, giving the Jewish baby to the Palestinian mother and the Palestinian baby to the Jewish mother. In their new identities, they must come to terms with their prior actions and views.

Only if we can make our peace with the actions taken in our (hypothetical) other identity can we say that we are moral in thought and deed.

Another important point is that I don't know whether or not human life has inherent meaning. I do think that each of us, within the context of our predetermined life circumstances, endows his or her life with meaning - for him/herself and for those around him/her - through his/her actions. Here is where we have the choice of the direction our lives and actions will take in the context of these imposed circumstances. Everyone is faced with the choice of whether to be a part of a predefined mainstream or to think for him/herself and to independently evaluate what's going on around him/her and act accordingly. We are all presented with a variety of values and objectives, and must often choose among them. Moral values and the choices based on them often clash with the others. Each person must choose whether to give in to social pressure and suspend one's own moral judgment as regards one's identity group or to risk his/her position in the group by standing up for personal moral choices.

"YOU AND THOSE LIKE YOU ARE TRAITORS!"

We peace and human rights activists try to live up to the moral standards I have alluded to, and to apply the principles of morality and justice to everyone, not only to our own identity group, but also to those outside it, including our enemies.

We are not willing to let allegiance to our own group obscure our moral judgment. One must remember that, thanks to such allegiance, coupled with moral blindness towards the enemy or others who do not belong, leaders throughout history have been able to convince those under their sway to commit the most heinous crimes against humanity. Mankind is its own worst enemy, more so than disease, predators, natural disasters, and accidents.

Because of our refusal to suspend moral judgment, many on the political right and center regard us as traitors. They claim that we care about the enemy more than our own people. The problem with this is that what they're actually saying is that our nation-state is inherently disrespectful of human rights and peace. For, if fighting for human rights means being a traitor, then the state is, in essence, against human rights. If fighting for peace means being a traitor, then the state is against peace. I am certain that many of those who label us as traitors don't really mean to imply this.

Our situation is similar to that of whistleblowers who expose corruption in their workplace. First of all, they report their discovery to their superiors. When those in charge don't take care of things, they turn to the police and media in hopes that these will help put an end to the corruption. Their actions earn the respect of the general public, but in their workplace (their "identity group"), they are considered traitors for exposing internal matters to the outside world. In most cases, they end up out of a job. Like peace and human rights activists, these whistleblowers value their own moral judgment over allegiance to their identity group. And despite having fought for their workplace, whose very survival may have been threatened by corruption, they are perceived by their colleagues as traitors for washing the company's dirty laundry in public.

NOT WANTING TO KNOW

Our "identity groups" demand that, in order to demonstrate our allegiance to the group, we suspend moral judgment so we can continue to belong. Indeed, most people choose not to know about or to fight against immoral activity, so as not to subject themselves to the conflict between group loyalty and moral judgment and find themselves marginalized or even ousted from their society. If knowledge of criminal actions by our own group does come to light, all possible justifications are immediately trotted out. Also, like most whistleblowers, we peace activists do not act out of a sense of morality, alone; we are concerned, as well, for our own security and survival should peace not be achieved and hostilities continue.

The majority of Germans did not know nor wish to know about the Nazi crimes against Jews and others who were being murdered in their extermination factories during the Second World War. And to this day, Turkey refuses to acknowledge the genocide it committed against the Armenian people during and after the First World War. I witnessed this same attitude in the Communists who were willfully oblivious of the crimes that Communist regimes committed against their own subjects (Finally in 1956, at the 20th Congress of the Communist Party of the Soviet Union, Khrushchev spoke about the crimes of the Stalin era and allowed them to be acknowledged). Similarly, I see how most Israelis neither know nor wish to know about the crimes that Israel commits against its minorities and the Palestinians in the Occupied Territories. In all of these cases, however, everyone is quite well informed about crimes of which they themselves were the targets.

MORALITY VERSUS INSTINCT

This causes me to reflect upon the problematic nature of morality. Here we have a tool that is supposed to prevent mankind from going so far as to destroy itself, while making it possible for human beings to establish and live in well-regulated societies. Yet all too often, it doesn't function this way, and is unable to keep murderous instincts at bay. Morality is, after all, one of the things that differentiate human beings from the other animals. Every species of animal has instincts that ensure its survival, even when there are clashes between individuals or groups within that species - instincts that put a check on the stronger party's aggressiveness when the weaker one shows signs of surrender, thereby usually preventing intra-species killing.

We humans, too, have ways of signifying surrender, which are meant to save the life of the one who's losing the fight, but unlike the other animals, we have a choice whether to acknowledge them or not. Moreover, much of the time, the loser is killed before having had a chance to signal submission.

As I understand it, this is the reason that once humans had learned to use tools and weapons, instincts ceased to be a reliable way of preserving the species. They had evolved to deal with the physical power bestowed upon living beings by nature. Weapons introduced a new dimension of force to human fighting that instincts weren't designed to handle. What was now required was a different mechanism that would take over the role of instincts in preventing the self-destruction of the species. This is where morality comes into play.

The problem is that instincts aren't a matter of choice; they impose themselves upon the living being, forcing it to act in accordance with their dictates. Not so morality, which is rational, and allows us to choose whether to follow it or other considerations. So it seems to me that today, man's greatest enemy is himself; mankind, with its modern weaponry, is more capable than natural disasters, disease, accidents, and predators put together of bringing about the extinction of the species.

Here is precisely where peace and human rights movements the world over endeavor to provide a counter-weight to the dangers posed to the survival of the human race by the development of modern weaponry. Where morality has repeatedly failed, these movements attempt to provide the missing element by insisting on the importance of extending moral considerations beyond one's own group to include the enemy. True, it angers our people - not only Israelis, but any people - when we demand moral and just treatment for our enemies, even while they are threatening or actively harming us. For most of us, our first impulse is the desire to destroy our enemies. We saw the most extreme expression of this urge in the case of Nazi Germany. We see it in all of the genocides that have taken place throughout human history. We see it in the massacres committed time and again. Anyone who stands in the way is simply killed; moral precepts no longer apply to him/her. The greater the fire power in the hands of the perpetrators of these mass murders, the greater the threat to the survival of the human race and perhaps of all living things on the face of the earth. It is when confronted with such dangers that the peace and human rights movements attempt to impose limits--so that we may survive into the future.

We in the Israeli peace and human rights movement naturally focus on our own conflict, but when similar movements elsewhere are examined, we see that the same precepts guide both them and us. We, in our struggle for Israeli-Palestinian and Israeli-Arab peace, are an integral part of the universal struggle for the survival of the human race, to which wars pose such an enormous threat.

We need to ask: What actually happens in cases of massacres and genocide; what allows them to take place and what prevents them? Here, I'm afraid, lies a dangerous mine field. I'm just sharing some thoughts, certainly not making any authoritative declarations. Take two well-known cases of mass murder, by the Nazis and by Communist regimes. These are two very opposing ideologies. One venerates nature, as it understands it; the other strives to create an ideal society that would ensure an egalitarian existence for all human beings. The Nazis took theories of racial supremacy, which were widely accepted in their days, to the extreme. They incarcerated their domestic opponents in concentration camps and did away with many of them, rendering local opposition to their actions weak and ineffectual. Meanwhile, the countries that were fighting them concentrated on winning the war, not on putting an end to the slaughter, so there was really no one to prevent the Nazis from carrying out their "final solution" until they lost the war.

It's more difficult for me to understand what brought about the mass murders that took place in the context of Communist revolutions. This is something that occurred during the French Revolution, as well, albeit apparently on a smaller scale.

Here we have world reformers on their way to fulfill their lofty vision, abandoning all moral and ethical inhibitions that might prevent them from murdering masses of their own people, on the pretext that they are doing it "for the revolution." Their wonderful vision has obliterated their moral inhibitions, their actions made easier by their invocation of a "scientific" theory promising the realization of that vision: a classic case of belief in the well-known maxim that "the end justifies the means." Here too, terrorist acts against opponents weakened internal resistance to their actions. Those who shared their vision from afar, or at least some of them, found it hard to believe that people with such lofty aims were capable of such horrifying deeds. The rest apparently accepted the suspension of moral and ethical standards out of agreement with that time-worn maxim.

These events underscore the importance of separating vision and justice from the ethics of war[1] - an ethic that should be effective and binding regardless of the justness or importance of the objectives being fought for.

Thus we see that in the absence of effective internal and external resistance, the danger of genocidal war increases. When I hear the anger directed, in Israel, at peace and human rights organizations that interfere with actions by the army and the state against the Palestinians, I realize all the more how important these groups are in limiting the danger that Israel might launch a devastating war against the Palestinians and the rest of its enemies. I feel similarly when I hear the anger expressed towards the UN Human Rights Commission and the fear that it could bring charges against Israel at the International

---

1   see the essay, "The Ethical Question," p 117

Court of Justice in The Hague, or towards countries that pressure Israel to desist from the committing war crimes and from tightening its grip on the Occupied Territories. In all of these cases, one can clearly see the importance of pressure from outside the country in reducing the danger of genocidal war. For example, it is this outside pressure that compels the army to consult legal experts for advice as to what is allowed and forbidden according to International Law, when attacking Palestinian targets.

If we think about the legitimacy granted to the establishment of an army and police force that are empowered to operate outside the bounds of morality, we can see that this is where the danger of genocidal wars originates. Such wars have their roots in the lifting of the moral constraints against mass murder. This highlights the importance of the ethics of war in reducing the threat of mass murder, as well as the importance of striving to end all war.

NUCLEAR ARMS

Nuclear armaments have introduced a new dimension of inconceivable destructive power, confronting us with the question of whether our moral and ethical systems are capable of coping with it. We're speaking here about the ability to cause a degree of destruction and death that reveals the paradoxical nature of the entire concept of the use of force to resolve conflicts. The producers of nuclear weaponry hope it will give them absolute security. This kind of absolute security, however, gives rise to absolute insecurity! When one side in a conflict equips itself with nuclear arms, the other side makes efforts to do likewise. And if nuclear war breaks out, mutual annihilation is imminent, with the added danger that the entire human race could be obliterated and with it all other forms of life on earth. One must ask: Can our planet survive such a war? As Martin Luther King Jr. once said: "The choice is not between nonviolence and violence. The choice is between nonviolence and non-existence."

Let us turn our attention to an interesting phenomenon that has been observed in the case of nuclear arms: The nuclear powers avoid using them in the wars they wage, apparently reserving their use for clear threats to their own survival. They also have so far refrained from engaging directly in warfare amongst themselves. Instead, they support and collaborate in wars conducted by their allies against allies of the other side, as was the case in Vietnam, for instance. Nonetheless, it is important to remember certain cases where we came perilously close to nuclear war, as during the Cuban missile crisis, when a Soviet submarine found itself being pursued by an American warship. Out of contact with Moscow and fearing that they were at war, the sub's captain wanted to launch a nuclear torpedo. However, doing this required agreement by all three chief officers, one of whom insisted that it not be done. Only due to this officer's stubbornness was this potentially devastating action (and the inevitable repercussions that would have followed) prevented.

All of this is in addition to the constant danger that nuclear war might break out as a result of human error or technological malfunction.

Each side in the Israeli-Palestinian/Arab conflict would like to completely eject the other from the area. We fear that the Arabs want to "throw us into the sea" – in other words, put an end to our existence here. On the other hand, without saying it in so many words, Israel denies the validity of the Palestinians' presence between the River Jordan and the Mediterranean Sea. We can see this in the ongoing process of pushing them off their land, which doesn't pause even when the negotiations of the so-called peace process are taking place. This is a conflict where the threat of full-blown war is particularly great, which also increases the likelihood that nuclear arms might be used.

Wars of annihilation have taken place throughout history, and many peoples and tribes have been wiped out as a result. But until recently, these conflicts were not conducted in the shadow of nuclear weapons. Thus, in spite of the terrible devastation they involved, they were not able to wipe out the entire human race and life in general. Our own conflict **is** taking place in the shadow of nuclear weapons, and Israel is widely regarded to be the only Middle Eastern power to possess them. Naturally this encourages those on the other side to try and acquire their own nuclear arsenals, as well as other weapons of mass destruction, making it all the more urgent to achieve peace between us and the Arab world before it's too late! It also underscores why it is so important for the rest of humanity to intervene in order to bring about the conflict's culmination in a peace settlement.

PART 2

TO UNDERSTAND THE CONFLICT

HUMAN RIGHTS VIOLATIONS IN THE SERVICE OF EXPANSIONISM

A very large proportion of the human rights violations that Israel commits in the Occupied Territories, as well as inside Israel proper, serve its expansionist policies and the takeover of Palestinian land. To explain this, I wish first to describe how I understand the Israel-Arab /Israeli-Palestinian conflict.

This is one of those conflicts that arise when one society invades the living space of another and, over time, systematically takes it over, while forcing the indigenous population out altogether or into an ever-shrinking piece of territory. The invaders, having the technological and organizational advantage, are able to prevail over the more numerous locals. Other examples are the incursions by Europeans in the Americas, Australia, South Africa, etc.

Naturally, these all took place under differing historical circumstances and evolved differently, but in every case, the invaders possessed technological and organizational advantages that gave them the military advantage. In addition, the arrival of numerous immigrants facilitated the takeover of the land, while the colonists received strong support from abroad.

In South Africa, where the pool of potential immigrants was small, the native Africans eventually managed to halt the process of expulsion and to change the ruling situation, transforming the society through a process of de-colonization, thanks largely to growing resistance world-wide to racism and human rights violations. In this context, the sanctions on South Africa were crucial, not so much because of their economic effect, but rather because of their role in eroding outside backing and support for white supremacist rule. At the same time, South Africa's black population had a large body of natural supporters that grew in strength as more and more whites began to lend their support.

There is an important lesson here for Israelis: The continued occupation and ongoing expulsion of Palestinians constitute a grave threat to support for Zionism internationally and put Israel's continued survival at risk. The reserve of potential Jewish immigrants is dwindling at any rate. Only if Israel ceases its ongoing oppression of the Palestinians and returns to its pre-1967 borders will it be able to regain this support.[2]

As mentioned above, since the beginning of Zionist immigration to this region, we have witnessed one society invading the habitat of another and systematically, over time, pushing the other group out. This is the core of the conflict. Here are some data to illustrate my point:

Prior to the commencement of Zionist immigration to Palestine, Jews constituted ten percent of the local population, living mainly in the cities of Hebron, Jerusalem, Tiberias, and Safed. I estimate they possessed less than one percent of the land. After 66 years of Zionist immigration and land purchas-

---

2   (See also: "The Nature of the Conflict," p. 154)

es, just prior to the 1948 founding of the State of Israel, Jews constituted one-third of the local population and owned only 7-8% of the land. During the 1948 war, most of the Palestinians were either expelled or fled the country. During and following the war, large numbers of Jews were brought in and in parallel, widespread takeover and theft of land was carried out. At present, Jews make up nearly 75% of the population inside Israel and control 96% of the land. The Palestinians constitute 20% of the population and hold 3.3% of the land.

And it didn't stop there. During the occupation that followed the conquest of June 1967, we have seen the same process at work. Currently, 57% of the West Bank lands (not including East Jerusalem) are in Israeli hands. Some 400,000 Jewish settlers live amongst about 2,700,000 Palestinians. In East Jerusalem, Israel holds over 40% of the land, and about 220,000 settlers live in the midst of about 320,000 Palestinians.

In the Golan Heights - occupied in 1967 - about 18,500 settlers now live alongside 25,000 Syrians. An estimated 80% of the land there is in Israeli hands. So we see that the process of taking over the country is still in full swing.

Israel takes control of territory by acquiring (through purchase or by force) land and pushing Palestinian Arabs into smaller and smaller areas or out of the country entirely. Prior to the establishment of the state, land purchase had become a major means of takeover. During the months of hostilities that preceded the declaration of the State of Israel in May of 1948, and subsequently, forcible takeover became the rule. To that end, legislation was passed as needed to provide the legal underpinning for immoral acts involving blatant violations of human rights. Time and again in these contexts, we see a clash between law and morality and between law and human rights.[3]

The utilization of legislation to implement human rights violations goes even further. Inside Israel, planning and construction laws are manipulated to deprive a large proportion of the minority (i.e., Palestinian Arab) population of the opportunity to build legally. Similarly, in the name of "law enforcement," every year the state denies hundreds of families in Israel their basic human right to shelter by declaring their dwellings illegal and demolishing them. Interestingly, nearly all of these families are members of the Bedouin Palestinian minority.

The same thing goes on in the Occupied Territories, where Israel has taken the planning and construction committees away from the local civil authorities and placed them under military jurisdiction. Naturally, these committees hardly ever issue building permits, which forces many Palestinians to go ahead and build without permits. Then along comes the very same authority, enforces the "law", and demolishes hundreds of dwellings every year.

Pre-state land purchases, too, involved the violation of human rights - in this case those of Palestinian tenant-farmers. The Effendi (owner of the land) who sold the land would evict the tenants and hand over the (now empty) land to the Jewish buyers. Since the founding of the state, these violations of human rights have mostly been committed by force. Following 1948 War land takeover was accomplished by preventing the return of refugees to their homes and land, as well as by outright confiscation and by declaring entire areas State Land. The

---

3   (See also: "Utilizing the legal system" p. 125).

greater part of the landholdings of Palestinians in Israel thus passed from Arab to Jewish hands. An important aspect of this story was Israel's exploitation of the fact that many Palestinians had never registered ownership of their properties with the Ottoman Land Registry. This allowed the state to steal it outright, since traditional forms of land ownership were simply not recognized; only registration with the Ottoman authorities was accepted as legitimate.

In the Negev (Israel's southern desert), along with the expulsion of Bedouin from the country (which continued until 1959), Israel began to concentrate them in the Sayag Zone (reserve - in the north-eastern Negev). The state then proceeded to take over the vacated land, passing the required laws as needed. At the end of the sixties, Israel instituted a policy of relocating the Bedouin in "planned towns" in order to seize the little they had left. This was accompanied by theft of their lands, as well as limitations on grazing, both of which had a negative impact on their ability to make a living or follow their customary way of life. Because a large part of the Negev Bedouin population has refused this forced concentration, the state denies their villages' official recognition and, on top of that, basic services such as running water, electricity, roads, etc. As well, homes are demolished, crops are destroyed, and herds confiscated - in hopes of persuading their owners to move into the planned towns. All these are violations of human rights intended to push the Bedouin off their landholdings, which are then handed over to Jews.[4]

---

4   (See also: "The Case of the Negev Bedouin," p. 134.)

The massive land-grab from the Palestinians who remained in the country after the establishment of the state and became Israeli citizens severely harmed their ability to support themselves from agriculture and forced most of them to seek employment in the Jewish sector. Yet, any time that Palestinians resist being systematically driven off their land, Israelis regard this as a threat to their security. Here again, human rights are being violated in the name of "'security".

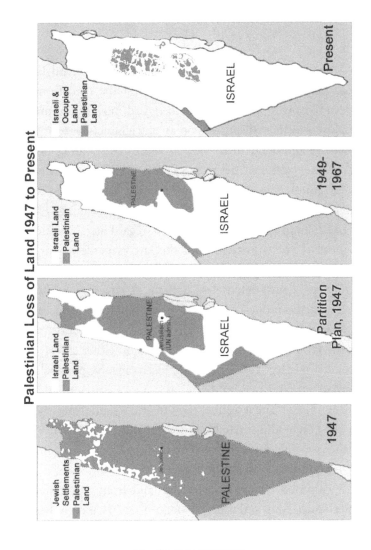

Credit: MAPPORN

HOW WAR IS UNDERSTOOD

No one gives up their land and home willingly. And Israel is waging a never-ending battle to wrest the land from its Palestinian Arab inhabitants, who regard most of the means employed in their dispossession as outright acts of war. This reflects a profound difference in the understanding of the term "war" by the parties to this conflict. Most Jewish Israelis understand war as a violent confrontation between two sides, whereas for Palestinians, "war" has a broader meaning.

Land confiscation, which the Jews regard as a bureaucratic measure for enforcement of the law, is perceived by the Palestinians as a unilateral act of war waged by the occupying power against defenseless civilians. A government official arrives at the property in question and issues a confiscation order to its owner. If he doesn't meet him, he lays the document on the ground under a stone and leaves. In either case, this is a totally "passive" event, in that it doesn't involve physical violence or casualties - even though it can take place only thanks to the implicit threat against the life of the landowner should he insist on holding on to his property. This kind of event - one of the principal ways of transferring land from Palestinian to Jewish control - is an essential aspect of the conflict.

A common way of transferring land from Palestinian to Jewish ownership and use, is to declare it as what is euphemistically referred to as "State Land." This is yet another example of how the occupiers use the legal system to the transfer of Palestinian land to their exclusive use. The Israelis regard this as a legal activity necessary for the regulation of land status. For Palestinians, it is a unilateral act of war by the occupying authority against defenseless civilians.

House demolition is both extremely traumatic and highly visible. First, large segments of the populace are prevented from building their homes legally, so they are forced to build without permits. Next, a demolition order is issued, plunging the entire family into a state of anxiety. Then the military (in the Occupied Territories) or police (within Israel proper) arrive and eject them from the house. Finally the demolition contractor (Believe it or not, there are people who do this for a living!) arrives and demolishes it before their very eyes. For Israelis this is law enforcement. For Palestinians, it is a unilateral act of war on the part of a military force against defenseless civilians, destroying not just their homes, but also their lives; an act of violence that traumatizes not only its direct victims but also the neighbors who witness it.

Eviction from one's home and land is another highly traumatizing act that takes place both in time of war as defined by both sides, and when things are quiet, or "peaceful", in terms of the Israelis' definition of war. In "quiet" times, this tactic is employed especially against vulnerable populations such as Bedouins or people living in expanding villages in their far-away lands. Generally the area is declared a military zone (some areas have even been declared nature reserves or archeological sites for this purpose), and the villages there are pronounced illegal. The military or police arrive and evict the people. If sufficient pressure is exerted by peace and human rights organizations in Israel and abroad, the inhabitants are not expelled outright. Instead, their homes, sheep and goat pens, storehouses, and cisterns are demolished; access roads are blocked, property is confiscated, depriving them of their means of livelihood, until they leave "voluntarily." The Jews regard this as law enforcement. The Palestinians see it as unilateral acts of war by the military authorities against defenseless civilians.

Jewish settlements in the Occupied Territories are built on land stolen from Palestinians. Usually the planning schemes for these settlements provide for massive expansion, which gives some indication of the state's intentions for its settlement project. The "moderate" settlements, once established, begin a relentless process of stealing land from their neighbors for purposes of expansion. This is usually justified on the grounds of the settlers' need for security (What about the security needs of Palestinians?!). In the "extremist" settlements, settlers start right in attacking those of their Palestinian neighbors whose fields are closest to the settlements. Little by little, they chase the Palestinians away and take over their land. It is interesting to note that Israeli soldiers do not stop the assailants. After all, their job is to protect them. Israeli police don't catch the assailants either, most of the time. If, despite this, they are still caught and brought to trial, the judiciary generally takes their side and acquits them. In the few cases where they do end up in jail, it turns out that their jailers are most compassionate. And in most cases, the president of Israel, too, proves to be a merciful soul and grants them pardons.

Of course, some settlements are illegal even by Israeli law. These are the so-called "outposts" erected on Palestinian land without the permission of the government, or even in contravention to official decisions. A 2005 report by former head of the State Prosecution Criminal Department, Talia Sasson, on the outposts revealed that many of them enjoy government funding. The Israeli army provides security and paves roads for them. Nor do they have any problems obtaining adequate water or electricity. After a few years of illegality, they receive official recognition. . . .

All of the above are unilateral acts of war waged by an occupying power against defenseless civilians. And there's more: Palestinians who have lived abroad for extended periods are often denied the right to return to the Occupied Territories; when residents of the Occupied Territories marry foreign nationals, the foreign spouses are compelled to enter the country as tourists, for limited periods of time only, in order to live with their families at all - a privilege that can be withdrawn at the whim of the authorities. Since the Population Registry remains under Israeli control, even in areas that the Oslo Accords of 1993 designated as being under the jurisdiction of the Palestinian Authority, the PA is not authorized to grant citizenship to these spouses. Again, this is a unilateral act of war by an occupying power against defenseless civilians.

By various estimates, Israel diverts some 80% of the water from the West Bank aquifers for the use of Israeli settlers and in Israel proper, dramatically reducing the amount available to Palestinians, at the same time that many wells and rainwater cisterns are being destroyed or rendered unusable. Again, a unilateral act of war by an occupying power against defenseless civilians.

The interesting thing about the examples I have cited - all of which fit the Palestinian definition of acts of war - is that they have nothing at all to do with Israeli security. These are acts undertaken solely in order to expand Israel's territory at the expense of the Palestinians. They contravene military ethics and infringe on human rights, and most of them violate international law, as well. In other words, Israel uses its army to achieve ends that not only don't make Israel more secure, they create the need for heightened security. If even the smallest percentage of the traumatized Palestinian victims of settlers and soldiers were to decide to take revenge on us Israelis for all that they have suffered, this would be sufficient to raise an "army" of terrorists eager to attack citizens of Israel.

Of course, when Palestinians attack civilians, they too are contravening the ethics of warfare and perpetrating war crimes. The Palestinians have no army to prevent the takeover of their land; they have no army to prevent the demolition of their homes; they have no army to prevent expulsions; they have no army to prevent the construction of settlements on their land; they have no army to enable the return of those who have been abroad for extended periods or the unification of "mixed" families; they have no army to prevent the theft of their water. In short, their security is almost completely nonexistent. (See "The Ethical Question" p.117)

All of this usually remains outside the discourse about the conflict. After all, it is a well-known fact that we Israelis have a constant need to defend ourselves. Palestinians' security requirements are not even an issue. Israel has managed to generate a discourse, both internally and internationally, based on a racist-colonialist paradigm whereby only Israeli Jews need security, and the Palestinians – the victims of Israel's expansionism – not only have no such need, they themselves are the security threat!

Most of the above-mentioned acts of war by Israel are carried out without fatalities. In the absence of bloodshed, the media show no interest and seldom report. Most fascinating of all, the majority of the Israeli, as well as international, media understand this conflict in the same way that most Israelis do. In other words, they have embraced the Israeli attitude toward security almost entirely, and thus largely refrain from reporting any of the practices I have listed. Thus, they did not see nor understand why the Second Intifada broke out in the midst of the Oslo "peace process." If the difference in the way the two sides perceive "war" is not understood, naturally any conception of the conflict itself will be distorted.

The Israeli military's role in providing security starts out with the need to suppress Palestinians' resistance to being evicted from their landholdings and expelled from their territory, and expands in response to the need to defend us against acts of revenge. Here is where the violations of Palestinian human rights in the name of Israeli security begin. Security also provides the pretext for seizing ever more land, expelling more Palestinians in the process, as witness the use of the Separation Barrier for this purpose. This is also evident when, in the name of protecting the settlements, more and more land is stolen from their Palestinian neighbors; and we see how the Israeli army jumps to the defense of settlers who attack Palestinian farmers working in their own fields - on land coveted for settlement expansion. All of this contravenes international conventions regarding the occupier's duty to provide security for the population under occupation. Another common ploy for taking over land and transferring it to Israeli ownership is to designate entire areas as army firing zones, expelling the

Palestinians who live there.

Also in the name of security, the army carries out night-time sweeps of Palestinian communities. Time and again we witness them arresting village activists who are struggling nonviolently to prevent the theft of their land. After many years during which not a single soldier has been killed in this context, it's obvious that this is not a matter of security, but yet another attempt to suppress Palestinians' efforts to hold on to their land - efforts which pose no threat to Israel.

SEEKING PEACE VS. DEMANDING JUSTICE

Countless times in debates with other Israelis over peace, I have been asked to show them the Palestinian Peace Now. Indeed, there is no such mass movement on the Palestinian side. After pondering the issue for some time, I asked them if they could show me an Israeli movement for Justice Now.

Just as the two sides show such deeply differing understandings of "war", they differ in their demands as to what should determine the shape of our shared future. When we Israelis speak of our aspirations for peace, we are really saying that we wish to secure the gains that we have made in this lengthy conflict. The Palestinians, by contrast, having lost most of their land, homes, and country, are demanding justice. They simply wish to restore that which has been taken from them.

Indeed, in the official peace talks (to the extent that they even exist), as well as unofficial ones (such as the Geneva Initiative), the Palestinians demand an end to the occupation; the dismantling of the settlements; the return of their land, water, and resources; return of the refugees; the restoration of East Jerusalem to Palestinian control. The radicals among them demand the entire land - from the Jordan River to the Mediterranean Sea. For the Palestinians, Israel proper, too, is occupied territory.

From this it is evident that when we speak about peace, we are referring to the outcome of a very painful compromise between the two sides, which would enable everyone to live together prosper in this land that is dear to us all. Therefore, it may indeed be more suitable to speak of a just peace.

We should note here the difference between reconciliation and peace. In the case of reconciliation, each side is able to live with the other's narrative. Peace, on the other hand, demands the making of painful compromises between these narratives. In fact, one of the ways that those who advocate the annexation of the Occupied Territories seek to undermine peace efforts is to make demands that are more appropriate to reconciliation, which have no chance of being accepted by the other side at this stage. For example, there is no way that Palestinians and Arabs in general would accept the Zionist project as justified. From their point of view, the problem of Europe's Jews should have been solved in Europe. They can neither understand nor accept why they must pay the price for the crimes that Christian Europe committed against its Jewish minority. In this connection, it's important to recall that the Zionist movement began in Europe as a reaction to Christian European anti-Semitism.

Similarly, there is no way that Israelis would agree to the negation of Zionism as a just cause, nor would they acquiesce to the demand to turn back the clock and restore things to their pre-1948 state.

THE LEFT'S UNAWARE INNER SPLIT

The differing demands of the two sides - peace versus justice - make me realize that in fact, activists on the Israeli left are divided into two camps, peace activists and justice activists. This requires us to make a very painful choice; both peace and justice are fundamental values that motivate us as leftists.

It's important to realize that one of the things that frighten the Israeli leadership away from truly entering into the peace process is the question of justice. One cannot demand the right of return for Jews after two thousand years in exile and at the same time oppose the right of return for Palestinians after 70 years, unless one is a nationalistic racist. The whole *raison d'etre* of Zionism was the establishment of a Jewish state. This is the reason that we are witnessing the expulsion of Palestinians, not only from specific pieces of land but from the entire territory. Under no circumstances would Israel accept a situation (e.g., return of a large number of Palestinian refugees) that would alter the demographics of the state in a way that would lead to the loss of its Jewish majority, and would commit collective suicide before allowing this. Therefore, if you are an Israeli peace activist, you are forced to give up on justice, and vice versa.

This is why I suggest that we speak about a fair solution rather than a just one. A fair solution means compensating all Palestinian refugees so that they can live in dignity and no longer as impoverished refugees.

Granted, when a peace activist denies the justice of the

Palestinian demand for the right of return, s/he is fundamentally contravening the demands of justice. After all, we Jews in Israel live here only thanks to the implementation of the Jewish right of return to this country. If you're not a racist, how can you justify denying the Palestinians the same right?

Given the cruel choice between peace and justice, I have chosen to be a peace activist, because only peace will put an end to Israel's expansion and the accompanying dispossession of the Palestinians. Only a peace that includes the establishment of a Palestinian state alongside Israel will force Israel to withdraw from the territories it occupied in 1967 and rein in its expansionist aspirations. And we mustn't forget that this whole discussion is taking place even as Israel's expansion continues. Every instance of land confiscation, every declaration of State Land, all of the house demolitions and other types of property destruction, the construction and expansion of settlements - and the many other measures that Israel constantly employs - are progressively expanding its area and forcing the Palestinians out. All of the acts of unilateral warfare that Israel continues committing are an extension of the catastrophe (*Nakba*) inflicted upon the Palestinians in the 1948 War – only now it is done slowly and mostly without fatalities, which helps to shield this ongoing process from public scrutiny.

There is a rather broad worldwide consensus in support of Israel's right to exist. This means there is almost no chance of achieving full justice for the Palestinians. It is for this reason that, in 1988, the PLO made its historic decision to embark upon a path towards peace with Israel. They did not cease to demand that justice be done, but realized that they would be compelled to compromise.

I recall the words of a Palestinian leader, Sufian Abu Zeida, in response to the question of how Fatah was different from Hamas. He said: "It took us in Fatah forty years to understand that we cannot force you out of the country, and there is no choice but – for the sake of the living – to make peace with you. We Palestinians do not have the additional forty years that it would take for Hamas to reach the same conclusion."

If the PLO has arrived at the painful realization that they cannot obtain justice and are therefore forced to choose the path of peace, then we Israeli leftists, too, must understand that under the current historical conditions, in choosing between the left's two fundamental values, we must opt for peace.

THE PROCESS OF EXPANSION IN THE OCCUPIED TERRITORIES

Immediately following the Six Day War in June of 1967, Israeli society was plunged into a debate regarding the future of the territories that they had just conquered. Opposing movements emerged, the one calling for a "Greater Israel," the other for "Peace and Security." The former advocated for annexation of the newly conquered territories by Israel, whereas the latter demanded that Israel be willing to relinquish them in exchange for peace.

Essentially the same debate persists to this day. Frequently in such debates, each side tries to portray its opponent's position in the most extreme manner possible and to thereby expose its paradoxical nature. Thus, the opponents of peace (i.e.., the proponents of Greater Israel) challenge the peace movement members: "Why return only the territories occupied in 1967? After all, the entire country is 'occupied' (including the territory within the state itself). Return all the rest as well!"

On the other hand, one of the major issues under debate is demography. Those who oppose annexing the occupied territories often claim that, over time, doing so would result in an Arab majority in Israel and put an end to the Zionist state. For supporters of annexation, it has been difficult to counter the demographic argument; only those on the extreme right have had the temerity to speak of the "transfer" of Arabs from the country. The memory of recent history, when German Nazis spoke of transferring the Jews out of Europe, has delegitimized the expression of such ideas in Israeli discourse.

In 1967, then minister of labor, General (res.) Yigal Alon came up with a plan that seemed somewhat of a compromise between the two approaches. He proposed, in the name of security of course, to annex some of the territories, while excluding the most densely populated parts of the Palestinian West Bank. Today we see that one outcome of the Oslo Accords has been to produce a kind of extended Alon plan, in that Israeli control has been extended to encompass settlements located precisely in the densely populated Palestinian areas. And we now see Israel making efforts to drive Palestinians out of Israeli controlled Area C into Palestinian controlled Areas A and B, in anticipation of the annexation of Area C, which would leave areas A and B as Palestinian Bantustans. Of course, all of this involves blatant violations of Palestinians' human rights.

This is already essentially the situation in the West Bank. With the Oslo Accords, Israel divested itself of responsibility for most of the population of the Occupied Territories and handed it over to the Palestinian Authority. The PA, in turn, is only able to function with the help of massive economic aid from Europe, the US, and the wealthy Arab states. This has created a situation wherein all of the donors to the PA are actually contributing to the Israeli occupation by freeing the occupier from its obligations to the occupied!

A similar situation prevails in the Gaza Strip. Israel has not handed control of the Gaza Strip to any governing body, so Hamas rule of Gaza has no political status. Yet, in effect, they govern Gaza under the aegis of Israel. So in Gaza, too, Israel has freed itself of its commitment to the population under occupation, while continuing to control the land, sea, and air space and to do with them as it pleases. Again, the donor states are enabling Israel to evade its responsibilities towards the local population.

Soon after the 1967 war, with Labor in power, a process of takeover and colonization of land in the Occupied Territories began, with the implementation of both governmental and nongovernmental initiatives. Most of the first settlements in the Golan Heights and the West Bank were nongovernmental; subsequently the Israeli army mobilized and began establishing Nahal strongholds (i.e., military settlements) in the Occupied Territories, which were turned over to civilian settlers a few years later. Not surprisingly, "security" was the pretext for establishing the settlements. At the same time, the Green Line (armistice lines of 1949) separating the State of Israel from the Occupied Territories was being erased from Israel's official maps. When the Yom Kippur War broke out in October of 1973, we witnessed the speedy (temporary) evacuation of the settlements in the Golan Heights, which clearly demonstrated that security had played no part in their establishment.

Note that Israel's borders, fixed by the ceasefire agreements in 1949, are problematic as far as international law is concerned. Borders between states are recognized only when both sides agree to them. Israel's borders were established in ceasefire agreements and not in political agreements between the sides. Still all the states that recognize Israel did so, waiving convention, within these borders. As soon as Israel itself refuses to recognize them as its borders, a ridiculous situation ensues whereby Israel does not recognize Israel! Moreover, as soon as Israel reopens the question of its borders in order to expand them, it runs the risk of facing a demand to go back to the partition lines decided upon by the UN in November of 1947. This same world consensus around the ceasefire lines of 1949, which Israel opposes, bolsters the claims of the Palestinians – realizing that they cannot remove Israel altogether – regarding the borders of their future state. Israel naturally rejects even this - all on account of its unspoken policy since the 1967 war of expanding its territory, even though this increasingly puts its existence and security in jeopardy. This raises the question: What is more important for the governments of Israel, territorial expansion or retaining our existential security?

Importantly, Israel's peace agreements with Egypt and with Jordan created borders that are agreed-upon, and thus recognized under international law, so that at present, Israel's southern borders are indeed recognized.

Thus we have, regressed to the practices of pre-state days, when the Zionist movement was creating "facts on the ground" as a prelude to the establishment of the State of Israel. Again, a new reality is being forged in violation of international law, and often even of Israeli law, all with the goal of creating facts "on the ground" culminating in the annexation of additional territory. All of this continuous, hectic activity again raises the question: If the State of Israel wanted to expand its territory, why did it not do so all at once, rather than by dribs and drabs; and why hasn't it declared its' intentions openly and officially?

SUPPORT BY WORLD POWERS AS A NECESSARY CONDITION FOR THE FULFILLMENT OF THE ZIONIST DREAM

In order to answer these questions, it is helpful to become acquainted with certain facts about Zionism:

From the outset, leaders of the Zionist movement realized that no one was just sitting there, waiting for them to come and take the land. They understood that the indigenous population would resist the invasion of their land and would not give it up willingly. That is why, from the very beginning, the Zionist leaders did their best to convince the rulers of the world powers of the day to support the Zionist project. The Balfour Declaration of 1917 was a significant consequence of that effort.

In this context, it should be noted that the prevailing myth, that Israel's independence was the result of a war against foreign (i.e., British) rule, is problematic. After all, had Britain not enabled the Zionist project at the expense of the indigenous population, the State of Israel could not have been founded in the first place. On the other hand, it is true that Britain - in response to Palestinian opposition and taking into consideration the terms of the Balfour Declaration (i.e., that the establishment of a homeland for the Jewish people in Palestine should not "prejudice the . . . rights of existing non-Jewish communities") - slowed the pace of Jewish immigration and reduced the numbers allowed entry into Palestine annually. It also attempted to place limits on the size of the future Jewish state. The struggle against foreign rule, then, arose from the fact that the British rulers were trying to properly implement the Balfour Declaration, which made the establishment of a Jewish national home in Palestine conditional on neither harming the local people nor violating their rights.

Even after the establishment of the state, the perception that the world powers' commitment to Israel's existence is a necessary condition for survival persists. It is said that "in politics, there is no free lunch," and of course no world powers support Israel purely because they are convinced of the rightness of Zionism. They support Israel when it serves their interests. Thus, we saw France backing Israel in the 1950s, when the former was keeping the Egyptian army busy and lessening its involvement in Algeria. Incidentally, this special relationship with France enabled Israel to develop its nuclear capacity. However, after France pulled out of Algeria, its interests in the Middle East changed. Now desiring improved relations with the Arabs states, France imposed an arms embargo on Israel just prior to the outbreak of the '67 War and ended their special relationship.

I must qualify my statement that "no world power supports Israel purely because it is convinced of the rightness of Zionism." Guilt over the Holocaust and the history of anti-Semitism, which, to a certain extent, made the Holocaust possible, play an important role in garnering support for Israel. Besides, it must be said that some of the European backing for Zionism was motivated by anti-Semitism. Quite a few European leaders may have secretly hoped that Zionism would rid Europe of its Jews. Naturally, no one in the colonialist era would have envisioned solving the "Jewish problem" on European soil.

It seems to me that the same process that led to the 1967 war ultimately brought about the ramping up of the level of Israel-US relations to their present "special" status.

We must recall that this was the era of the cold war between the US and the USSR. The Arab Middle East was divided into spheres of influence of these two world powers: Egypt and Syria were pro-Soviet, whereas Jordan, Saudi Arabia, and the Emirates were pro-American. During the 1960s civil war in Yemen, Egypt sent in troops to support the anti-monarchist forces. From a US perspective, the presence of a pro-Soviet army on the Saudi Arabian border constituted a clear threat to its oil resources. Meanwhile, as the conflict between Israel and Syria over borders and water heated up, the Syrians appealed for help, and it's ally Egypt responded by redeploying some of its forces from Yemen to the Sinai Peninsula, a significant step in the escalation that culminated in the 1967 war. The Americans regarded this as a case of Israel tying up a pro-Soviet army and keeping it away from Saudi oil. Just as Israel had previously kept the Egyptian Army pinned down in the Sinai Desert, thereby preventing its intervention in Algeria, Israel was now diverting forces otherwise liable to attack the pro-American oil states. It has often turned out that these very same forces are being paid handsomely by the oil states not to attack them, which suggests that perhaps the US may have an interest in prolonging the Israeli-Palestinian conflict, by virtue of which Israel keeps those who might otherwise menace the oil-producing countries in the region out of the picture.

The events of September 1970 provide an additional example of Israeli actions in support of American interests in the region. The PLO had created a military force inside the pro-American

Kingdom of Jordan. The Jordanian regime could not tolerate a military force not subject to its control within its territory, and fighting broke out between the Jordanian army and the PLO. Pro-Soviet Syria prepared to invade Jordan in support of the PLO. Israel threatened to invade Jordan if Syria did so. Thus was a Syrian invasion averted. Again serving American interests.

Another such instance took place during Jimmy Carter's term as US president. Carter had decided to halt the sale of arms to countries with poor human rights records. In the cold war context of the times, there were those in the American administration who feared that these states might turn to the USSR for arms purchases and so transfer their allegiance from the US to the Soviet bloc. Israel sold them arms in an effort to prevent this.

In the run-up to the First Gulf War (1991), the Americans built a coalition that included Arab states such as Saudi Arabia, Egypt, Syria, and the Emirates. Iraq attacked Israel with missiles, hoping to provoke a reaction. The idea was that an Israeli attack against Iraq would result in the other Arab states deserting the US-led coalition, since they would not be willing to fight an Arab state that was under Israeli attack. The US pressured Israel to refrain from launching a counter-attack. And indeed, the very right-wing Israeli government behaved like a bunch of pacifists and did not respond to the missile attack - all in the name of not harming American interests.

It is in this context that I understand the peace treaty between Israel and Egypt. In the 1970s, Egypt began shifting its political orientation from pro-Soviet to pro-American. Part of the payment by the US for Egypt's transfer of allegiance was US pressure on Israel to withdraw from the Sinai Peninsula in exchange for peace with Egypt. Israel's then prime minister, Menachem Begin, leader of the right-wing Likud party and a staunch advocate of "Greater Israel", had to make the difficult choice between his ideology and Israel's special relationship with the US. Begin preferred to preserve this special relationship.

ZIONISM TODAY: SURVIVALISTS VS. ZEALOTS

In contrast to her party's leader, Geula Cohen, a Likud Knesset member at the time, thought that it was more important for Israel to hold on to the Sinai than to maintain its special relationship with the great world power, the US. She resigned from the Likud and founded a new party, *Ha-Tehiya* (The Revival), thereby exposing the significant difference between the two major trends in Zionism in relation to this issue: a Zionism dedicated to Israel's survival and one more akin to the biblical Zealots. The first of these sees Israel's alliance with the western powers as being a necessary condition for its ability to survive in a region where it is unwanted. To that end, survivalist Zionists takes pains to consistently serve the interests of these powerful allies - the US above all. Whenever a choice must be made between territorial expansions and maintaining this alliance, the alliance takes priority.

For modern-day Zionist Zealots - a group comprising mainly religious nationalists - the Occupied Territories is the top priority, and they will not give them up, even at the cost of global isolation and of putting Israel's very survival at risk. I consider the religious among this brand of Zionists to be true heirs of the Second Temple Zealots and their ilk, who were responsible for the destruction of the Second Temple.

The Romans who destroyed the Temple and exiled the rebels also allowed Yohanan Ben Zakai to found a Jewish study center in Yavne. It is clear, then, that they fought against those who rebelled against their rule, but had no quarrel with

Judaism as such. There, too, the two trends in Judaism clashed: the "survivalists" realized that they no longer had any chance of winning their fight against the Romans, and preferred to surrender, as long as this would allow them to survive and hold on to their Temple. The Zealots prioritized valor over survival. For them, the continued existence of the Jewish people would only be worthwhile if the Roman occupation were to end. Had every Jew adopted their approach, Judaism would no longer exist today.

What is both interesting and troubling is that survival-oriented Zionism - in seeking nationalist myths with which to buttress the revival of Jewish nationalism in Israel - chose, among others, the story of Masada, the symbol most associated with the Zealots of old. In fact, what we are seeing today is a "hostile takeover" of the Likud (formerly the right wing of survival-oriented Zionism) by the modern-day Zealots. There are now influential Likud members, including members of Knesset, who are solidly in the Zealot camp and who have been successfully pushing out the more survival-oriented representatives and bringing in more of their own, many of whom don't even vote for the Likud on Election Day.

The first confrontations between the two brands of Zionists took place after the Occupation of 1967, when zealous members of *Gush Emunim* (the Bloc of the Faithful) began establishing settlements in areas with large Palestinian populations, that is, outside the limits stipulated by the Alon Plan (which determined the location of most settlements of the day). In most of these cases, the zealots overcame government opposition and succeeded in building their settlements. Confrontations over the establishment of *Gush Emunim* settlements ceased with the

Likud victory in the 1977 elections. With the Likud forming the government for the first time, it became much more obvious that the interests of the government ministers (most of whom were survival-oriented Zionists) and the zealots were essentially identical.

These two currents Zionism again clashed in the wake of the signing of the Oslo Accords in late 1993. I recall hearing a settler speaking on television at the time, saying that the government of Israel must decide: war against Arabs or war against Jews. The assassination of Prime Minister Yitzhak Rabin two years later painfully elucidated this dangerous divide. Shim'on Peres, who became prime minister following Rabin's murder, did everything in his power to downplay the controversy - providing us with what was apparently the only peace between Zionism's two political streams.

Incidentally, the right wing, in their struggle against Rabin, attempted to delegitimize him by labeling him a traitor. This is a highly dangerous tactic. If promoting peace means being a traitor, then as far as they are concerned, Israel is essentially against peace. And the most dangerous thing about using delegitimation as a weapon is that it is tantamount to calling for the spilling of blood: calling Rabin a traitor was like saying he was fair game. Unfortunately, the lesson has not been learned, and the charge of illegitimacy is still used against the Israeli left.

RESPONDING TO PEACE INITIATIVES WHILE AVOIDING PEACE

Israel's unilateral disengagement from Gaza led to yet another confrontation between the two currents of Zionism. Ariel Sharon (a survival-oriented Zionist), one of the most prominent proponents of Jewish settlement in the Occupied Territories, declared his acceptance of President Bush's 2003 Road Map for Peace, albeit with reservations. He then proceeded to undermine the Road Map by proposing unilateral disengagement from Gaza. Palestinian Authority President Mahmud Abbas (aka Abu Mazen) requested that Sharon agree to negotiate with the PA about leaving Gaza, and promised to do everything he could to ensure that Israel would not be attacked from Gaza. Sharon, fearing that negotiations would plunge him back into the peace process, refused.

He learned this lesson from Ehud Barak, his predecessor as prime minister. The latter, having caused the peace negotiations with Syria to fail, unilaterally withdrew the Israeli army from South Lebanon. And just as Israel's unilateral withdrawal from South Lebanon was taken by the other side as a triumph for "the resistance" and led to the strengthening of Hezbollah in Lebanon, Israel's unilateral disengagement from Gaza was no doubt also seen as a victory for "the resistance," in this case Hamas. In the end, this led to the strengthening of Hamas and the triumph of the hawks within Palestinian society. This made it easier for Israel to influence world public opinion, as it could now be portrayed as the side that gave up territory but did not receive peace in return; instead, it got rocket attacks on its inhabitants and rejection of peace.

This unilateral action, then, both kept the "danger" of peace at bay and shifted blame to the other side. Sharon - one of the greatest settlement builders - sacrificed the Gaza Strip settlements (displacing about 8000 Jewish settlers) and rid himself of responsibility for one-and-a-half million Palestinians within that small area. The entire exercise has been perceived as lessening the "demographic peril" and, because of the settlers' strong resistance, also gave rise to rather widespread opposition among the Israeli public to the idea of any future dismantling of settlements in the West Bank. Meanwhile, Prime Minister Sharon helped to create the impression that Israel would not be able to afford compensation to West Bank settlers on the scale that had been paid for the Gaza evacuation.

It is important to remember that following the death of Yasser Arafat, the Palestinians elected as their president Abu Mazen, who had objected to the violent intifada (uprising) and called for a "popular" intifada; i.e., without the use of violence. Abu Mazen is also considered one of the most moderate leaders of the Palestinian people. About a year later, following the unilateral disengagement from Gaza, Hamas won in the Palestinian parliamentary elections.

Both during and after the so-called "Oslo process," cooperation between the two trends of Zionism was maintained – as long as there was no effective pressure on the Israeli government to end the occupation.

Incidentally, Bush's Road Map seems to have been the most effective plan that the Americans came up in their efforts to bring us closer to peace, in that it required both sides to take steps towards resolving the conflict: Palestinian assurance of Israel's security in return for Israel's relinquishing the territories. This had the potential of revealing the truth that security concerns are not what are behind Israel's obstinate refusal to pull out of the Occupied Territories

Thus we see how every Israeli leader finds his own particular way of "responding" to peace initiatives, or redefining them - the main goal being to avoid a situation where Israel would have to surrender the Occupied Territories, while at the same time shifting the blame for the failure of peace efforts onto the Palestinians and diligently taking care not to damage Israel's good relations with the US and Europe.

CREATING FACTS ON THE GROUND

Just as in the days of the struggle against the British - who had, after all, enabled the Zionist project to take root and flourish in the country - Israel is once again changing the face of the country (by building settlements, roads, the wall...), in defiance of the official positions of the countries that give Israel the most support. This time, however, it is being done incrementally and with minimal bloodshed, so as to neither arouse their serious opposition to the ongoing territorial expansion nor harm the international relationships upon which Israel's continued existence is dependent.

Here, too, the old debate between the center-left and the right, dating back to pre-state times, resurfaces. Whereas the right wing laid out the aspirations of Zionism and articulated its objectives, the center-left advocated action over talk, and claimed that the right, with its declarations, was provoking Arab resistance to the Zionist project and sabotaging it. The left's slogan was "Another dunam (one dunam 1000 sq.m = 1/4 acre), another goat." Indeed we see that Israel's policy of territorial expansion was begun by the Labor government, in power after the 1967 War, on the pretext of "security considerations". Claiming that settlements were necessary for security, they (as mentioned earlier) had the Nahal ("Fighting Pioneer Youth") branch of the army set up military strongholds, which were later turned into civilian settlements.

To this day, the Israeli army diligently endeavors to avoid

fatalities in its day-to-day military operations against the Palestinian civilian population, such as house demolitions, theft of land and water, establishment of settlements, or expulsions. In this way they succeed in keeping this incessant low-level warfare out of the media spotlight and, as a result, Israelis and the rest of the world are barely aware of it. Keeping Palestinian fatalities to a minimum in this daily war also facilitates the perpetuation of the army's claim of "morality". Indeed, if you know nothing of the acts of war that the army commits every day against defenseless civilians, you might well believe its moral image. Here, as well, we can see the difference between the center-left and the right wing. The center-left is more concerned with concealing the expansionist policy from Israelis and the world at large, whereas the right is much more open about it. Interestingly, at least some of the right-wing Zealots have embraced the terms of the Oslo Accords, even as they continue to condemn them, and speak openly of their wish to annex Area C while leaving Areas A and B as Palestinian Bantustans.

THE CONTRADICTION BETWEEN ISRAEL'S PROTESTATIONS OF PEACE AND ITS ACTIONS ON THE GROUND

The Oslo Accords, which initially appeared to be an important breakthrough in the efforts to arrive at a historic compromise and peace with the Palestinian people, turned out to provide a telling example of Israel's strategy of appearing to pursue peace initiatives while at the same time intensifying the occupation.

The harsh confrontation between the survivalist Zionists and the latter-day Zealots in the wake of the Oslo Accords increased the degree to which the world - and Israelis - was being deceived about Israel's intentions. The Oslo Accords were, in fact, only interim agreements that did not impose a peaceful solution to the conflict (negotiations for a Final Status Agreement having been postponed to a later stage). In this interim period Yitzhak Rabin, observed how having power over a civilian population was corrupting the Israeli army and compromising its soldiers' capacity to fight. Therefore he was glad to pull the army out of Palestinian population centers, thereby freeing Israel from responsibility for the majority of the population of the occupied territories.

However, the land-grab continued. House demolitions continued. Expulsions continued. The settlement project expanded and became more entrenched. The theft of water received official sanction from the Accords, and so on and so forth. Thus, at a time when the Israeli public felt that the country was moving towards peace, on the ground, the war - as the Palestinians understand the term - continued unabated. During the seven years from the signing of the Oslo Accords in 1993 until the outbreak of the Second Intifada in 2000, Israel demolished about 1000 Palestinian homes in the occupied territories, evicted the entire population of several West Bank villages confiscated about 160,000 dunams (approximately 40,000 acres) of land, and nearly doubled the number of Jewish settlers in the West Bank, not counting East Jerusalem, from 110,000 to 204,000.

The terrorist attacks by Palestinians opposed to any compromise only made it easier for Israel to conceal its own policy of rejecting peace - from both its own citizens and the rest of the world. It is noteworthy that Ron Pundak – who did much of the groundwork preparing the way for the Oslo Accords – in an article marking twenty years since their signing, recounts that the negotiators asked Rabin and Peres for guidance as to the direction the negotiations should take. Regarding their response, he wrote: "Rabin and Peres left vague both the vision and the direction in which the negotiations should lead, making it clear that in any case a comprehensive two-state solution was not in the cards."

No place arouses people's sensitivities like the Temple Mount / Haram al-Sharif in Jerusalem, with its Muslim holy places. This fact is often exploited as a means of undermining peace efforts. We saw this in 1996, when the US President Bill Clinton was pressuring the first Netanyahu government to move forward towards an interim agreement with the Palestinian Authority, and Netanyahu authorized excavations to open the so-called Western Wall tunnel under the Temple Mount. Eighty people died in riots that ensued as the Muslim quarter's residents protested an action that they feared would cause the holy places above the tunnel to collapse.

Likud party leader Ariel Sharon's ascent to the Temple Mount in September of 2000, accompanied by several other Likud politicians and a large contingent of Israeli riot police, was another act intended to forestall any advance towards a peace agreement. When President Clinton offered his compromise proposal following the failure of the June 2000 Camp David meetings, Sharon took this action, thereby igniting the Second (or Al-Aqsa) Intifada. A few days prior to Sharon's provocative visit, Arafat had paid a visit to Prime Minister Ehud Barak, asking him to block it, and warning that it would result in uncontrollable riots. Barak played the democratic card, saying that he could not prevent Sharon's visit.

The Israeli government has also laid the groundwork for future provocations by transferring responsibility for archeological excavations in the Palestinian village of Silwan – thought by some to be the biblical 'City of David,' just outside the Old City walls – from the governmental Antiquities Authority to the Elad Association, whose declared aim is the Judaization of Silwan and the neighboring area. In so doing, the government knowingly handed over this extremely sensitive site to a private organization that I have reason to fear is affiliated with the Zealots.

The lesson I have learned from everything that took place in the territories from the signing of the Oslo Accords on September 13, 1993, until the outbreak of the Second Intifada in late September of 2000, is that one must always watch what Israel does on the ground rather than listen to its politically motivated declarations regarding its desire for peace. It's very clear: As long as settlements are the government's top priority; there will be no end to public funding of the settlement project; and construction will continue; no attempt has been made to encourage settlers to return to Israel proper; the land-grab continues; efforts to force Palestinians out of Israeli-controlled Area C are still in full force; the house demolitions continue; there has been no real effort to put an end to settler attacks on Palestinians; diversion of water for Israeli use has not ended; nor has Israel's interference with the Palestinian Population Registry of the West Bank. Thus, it is clear that Israel's government has no desire for true peace. Instead it carries on a deceptive discourse declaring its aspirations for peace while its actions in the occupied territories indicate the opposite.

AMERICA'S INTERESTS ARE WHAT COUNTS

In this context it's interesting to take a close look at the peace efforts between Israel and Syria. In the run-up to the first Gulf War, the US succeeded in recruiting Syria to its coalition against Iraq, along with several other Arab and Muslim states. These states complained that the US was fighting the Iraqi occupation of Kuwait but was doing nothing to end the Israeli occupation. The US response was to invite the foreign ministers of all the concerned countries (Syria, Lebanon, Jordan), to a peace conference in Madrid a few months after the war. Since Israel refused to permit the participation of the PLO, the Palestinian delegates from the West Bank and Gaza attended as part of a joint Jordanian-Palestinian delegation, but received their instructions from the PLO leadership. Israel's then prime minister, Yitzhak Shamir, not wanting to rely on his foreign minister, David Levy, represented Israel himself at the opening session. In the months that followed, both multilateral and bilateral negotiations were held between Israel and each of the participating Arab delegations.

The Rabin government, which replaced Shamir's in 1992, entered into negotiations with Syria. As far as is known, these negotiations made significant progress but no peace agreements were signed - as was also the case with the negotiations between Syria and Israel under Ehud Barak in 2000. We mustn't forget that Syria never changed its political allegiance, even after the fall of the Communist regime in the USSR, so that the US no longer had a real interest in effectively pressuring Israel to withdraw from the Golan Heights (captured from Syria in the 1967 war) - a Syrian condition for peace. This is also the reason for Russia's support of the Assad regime in the current civil war in Syria.

And it explains why the US is constantly coming up with initiatives for peace negotiations with the Palestinians in a "peace process" that doesn't actually result in peace. The Palestinians have no real capacity to serve American interests in a way that could lead to truly effective American pressure on Israel to pull out of the occupied territories. The US, initiates "peace efforts" in response to pressure from US-friendly Arab states - but does not impose them on Israel. This is the same reason that the mainstream Zionist lobby in the US has been so effective in averting any pressure on Israel. Only when it was clear that the US had an interest in Israel's achieving peace with Egypt, did the Zionist lobby not dare to oppose such pressure. After all, its activists are first and foremost American patriots. But since there is no obvious American interest in peace between Israel and the Palestinians - and perhaps even an interest in maintaining the state of war - the Zionist lobby can effectively prevent America from pressuring Israel to move towards peace.

THE TRANSFORMATION FROM IDEALISM TO HEDONISM

Some time in the seventies, a change took place in Israeli society, as in the world as a whole: a process of transition from an idealistically committed society to a hedonistic one. One obvious sign of this process has been the decline of socialism. In the late eighties and early nineties, we witnessed the fall of Communism and the dismantling of the USSR. We saw social democratic parties in many countries began to take part in dismantling the welfare state. And in Israel, first the *Moshavim* and then the *Kibbutzim*, abandoned their idealistic values and embraced privatization. In Israeli politics this was accompanied by the decline of the Labor party and the emergence of centrist parties based on transitory "stars" that vanished after a few terms in office at most.

We also saw this process at work in the protest movement for affordable housing that swept Israel in the summer of 2011 - whose leaders turned to university professors for help in defining their goals. At the same time, the influence of young people from secular *Kibbutz* and *Moshav* backgrounds in the Israeli army's combat units has been declining and that of graduates of the national-religious youth movement growing. This poses the danger that when the time comes, many such soldiers would obey their rabbis rather than the government, and we could find ourselves facing a civil war if a peace agreement is reached with the Palestinians. Anyone who is aware of the degree to which Zealots of today identify with

Yig'al Amir, Prime Minister Rabin's assassin, understands that Amir merely fired the first shots in the civil war that is liable to break out should the government dare to take real steps towards peace. In fact, one need only be aware of the gigantic budgets earmarked for the settlement project to realize that Israel's governments have been investing massive amounts of public funds in sowing the seeds for a future civil war.[5]

---

5   See also: "The rise and fall of the socialist movement," page 160

PART 3

SO WHAT DO YOU SUGGEST?

THE DIFFICULTIES FACING THE PEACE MOVEMENT AND THE HUMAN RIGHTS MOVEMENT

To reiterate what I wrote earlier (in the chapter entitled **"We're the Good ones!"**), the people who have taken issue with my point of view over the years have expressed the human need to see ourselves and the society with which we identify as "good." We're the "good guys" and our enemies are the "bad guys." However, a simple thought experiment will reveal that we Israelis would never tolerate the takeover of our land by descendents of one of the peoples who lived here prior to the invasion by the ancient Hebrews (according to the biblical account). I am certain that the great majority of Israelis would strongly reject such a scenario.

To reinforce my point, just look at Israel's treatment of African refugees, many of whom have fled the threat of genocide. They're not seeking to live here permanently, but only want a temporary refuge until the danger subsides. Yet Israel, a state of Holocaust survivors (and other refugees from oppression), is doing everything it can get away with under international law to bar their entry and to deport those who manage to get in.

Just as we wouldn't want to be displaced by descendents of, say, the ancient Canaanites, the Palestinians have never wanted the Zionists to come to their country and to force them out of their land. And neither the indigenous peoples of the Americas nor the Australian Aborigines wanted to be displaced by the Europeans. Morally, this is a terrible act: A group of people comes along, uproots the local population, and settles in their stead. The question remains: Even if they can justify this action to themselves, how can members of this group continue to regard themselves as good and moral and their victims as the "bad guys"?!

I can think of a number of mechanisms (there are, no doubt, many more) that make this possible:

1. Racism – in our case, I would call it national or religious racism.
2. Criminalization of the victim;
3. Legislation that portrays the injured party as the law-breaker;
4. Unwillingness to know, or denial of, what's actually going on;
5. Cover-ups;
6. Portraying one's own community as the victim;
7. "Everyone is doing it, so it's okay for us, too."

Racism in all its forms plays a key role in justifying the displacement of an indigenous population and its replacement by settlers from the dominant group. After all, what gives you more right to a certain territory than those who lived there before you? Only if the local inhabitants are regarded as inferior (e.g., not "promised this land by God"), could you do such a terrible thing.

The world's attitude towards racism changed drastically in the aftermath of World War II. The Nazis had merely taken to an extreme a worldview that was rather widely accepted at the time. One important lesson of WWII was that there is a moral imperative to combat racism. However, in our case, we saw ourselves not as being "racist," but as justified on national and religious grounds: "We have national rights to the land that supersede those of the indigenous population," or, "We were promised this land by God, and that supersedes the rights of the indigenous population."

Another mechanism for coping with the terrible act of dispossession, while continuing to view one's own side as "the good guys," is criminalizing the victims (the locals). "These terrorists have always wanted to wipe us out, so we are forced to defend ourselves." In every successful invasion, the invaders have had a significant military advantage over the locals. Thus, violent resistance by the local population, rather than endangering the invaders, reinforces their perception - and that of their supporters/ backers - of the locals as the ones in the wrong.

Regarding the criminalization of the victim, it is important to note the legislation that legalizes land-grabs and other modes of injustice inflicted upon the local population. Examples include planning and construction regulations under which a number of their communities and most of their buildings are rendered illegal, thereby enabling the systematic demolition of their homes and the criminalization of any who resist the theft of their land or who build upon it.[6]

Unwillingness to know what's going on is an important mechanism at play here. Most invaders simply do not wish to know about the damage done to the locals in their name. Those who

---

6 see the article, "How criminalization of the victim is done" p.147

do know mostly ignore it, and if pushed to where they can no longer ignore it, there are always excuses: "It's legal," "It's for our security," or "They are our enemies and this is the price they must pay for harming us"; "If they accepted our conditions, they would not be harmed."

Cover-ups are also important. Harm inflicted on the indigenous population is simply not reported, or is reported in a biased manner that whitewashes or justifies it. An interesting example of this is how the Israeli media consistently ignore the horrific home demolitions that Israel carries out even within its own borders, especially in the Negev, where some 1,000 homes are demolished every year. Alongside the demolition of the homes of Bedouin inside Israel, hundreds of dwellings are demolished each year in the occupied territories during periods of calm; in wartime this can reach thousands or even tens of thousands. And news of this destruction seldom reaches the public, or, if mentioned at all, it's tucked away on the inside pages of the newspapers.

Another very important mechanism is the portrayal of one's own group as the victim. That is, if we do not know what we are doing to the indigenous people, we don't see the connection between our actions and acts of revenge by our victims. After all, they are unable to prevent our incessant attacks, the goal of which is to drive them off what little land remains to them. Consequently, some of them turn to terrorism, which is a form of revenge for that which they cannot prevent. The Israeli "security" discourse is noteworthy here; that is, that all of the army's actions are carried out in the name of security: "We need to protect ourselves from those who are rising up to destroy us." All of this is viewed as unconnected to the actions of the army, which unfortunately have a large part in causing these terrorist acts.

Still another mechanism of self-justification is, "Everyone does it, so why should we be better?" "This is the way of the world; why should we be different?"

It's important to point out that many of the mechanisms I have mentioned are at play in other types of conflict as well, and are common to both sides of any conflict, since both sides always have a need to regard themselves as "the good guys" and their opponents as "the bad guys."

In order to maintain our self-perception as "the good ones," we invaders need to persuade our backers and supporters that this is indeed the case; without this support, Israel's existence would be in jeopardy. However, the Zionist invasion faces greater difficulties in convincing people this than those that preceded it. The invasions of America, Australia, and southern Africa took place in an era when technology did not facilitate such speedy information-dissemination as is possible today. They took place on the periphery of the known world of the day at a time when racism was widely accepted as legitimate. By contrast, the Zionist project is being implemented in a modern world where communication has become extremely rapid and people can travel amongst distant parts of the world within a few hours. On top of that, it is being carried out in an area that is sacred to all three monotheistic religions – one can almost say at it's the center of the world - and at a time when racism is no longer considered legitimate.

This makes it much more difficult for the Zionist invasion

than for its predecessors, and creates the need for obfuscation and the other mechanisms that I have cited above. Indeed, up until the twenty-first century, Israel managed to successfully hide its actions from the world and found it easy to present the terrorist acts carried out against it without reference to their context.

In recent years, largely thanks to right-wing Israeli governments that have tended far less to hide their deeds and intentions, a growing proportion of the populations of Western nations has begun to connect the dots between Israel's conduct and Palestinian terrorism. This has, of course, eroded Israel's global status and improved the Palestinians' chances of success. Now increasingly, people in the countries that are the principal sources of support for Zionist immigration are being exposed to another version of reality, very different from the one presented to them by Israeli propaganda. Furthermore, the more the level of Palestinian violence decreases and more Palestinians express a preference for nonviolent struggle, the easier it becomes for them to introduce their own narrative of the conflict to Western consciousness.

Through our activities, we on the left (peace and human rights movements) seek to undermine all of the above-mentioned mechanisms. We struggle against racism in the name of universal values of morality and justice. We oppose the criminalization of our victims. We oppose the legislation used to legitimize land-theft and discrimination and all of the other legislative manipulations practiced by Israeli regime to the detriment of its victims. We elucidate the connections between Israel's conduct and acts of revenge launched by terrorists against us. And, in the name of morality and justice, we reject the attitude that, "Everyone is doing it, so we may too."

These activities are important but they are also, unfortunately, responsible for the great difficulties in which the Israeli left – like the left everywhere – finds itself today. With every reference we make to human rights violations by Israel, and every time we publicize Israel's destructive actions, we attack Israelis' self perception that "We are the good ones, and they are the bad guys," the Israeli ear hears us saying, "We are the bad guys."… Similarly, when we say that in return for peace we must consider our enemies' demands and give back the occupied territories, we are depicted as caring more for our enemies than for our own people. It is important to point out that during periods of active conflict, it is all the more difficult for the majority of Israelis to hear our criticisms.

It is obvious from all I have said that the Israeli peace movement, like most peace and human rights movements the world over, confronts difficulties in its struggle for peace. Usually these movements are small opposition groups with little influence. I have long wondered why this is the case. After all, most humans do want peace. Only national, religious, or ideological fanatics who regard bravery and its glory as values superior to life itself (fascists) prefer war to peace. They usually are a small minority in human societies, and in most cases where they have acceded to positions of power, they have first imposed their rule on their own society, and only then attacked its enemies.

There have, of course, been instances where a peace or human rights movement became a mass movement and had some influence on the decision-makers. Such cases should be studied so as to understand what made them possible and what lessons we may learn from them.

SUCCESSES OF PEACE AND HUMAN RIGHTS MOVEMENTS

I can recall two occasions when the Israeli peace movement succeeded in having a sweeping influence within the general public. The first was after Egyptian President Anwar Sadat's historic visit to the country (1977). There was a sense at that time that then prime minister, Menahem Begin, meant to forfeit the chance of peace to his Greater Israel ideology. A group of reserve officers in the Israeli military got together and published an open letter calling upon Begin "to turn towards peace." One outcome of this was the creation of the Peace Now movement, which was able, for the first time in Israel's history, to organize massive demonstrations in favor of peace with Egypt

The second such instance was during the first Lebanon war (1982). Radical peace groups, later joined by Peace Now and many ad hoc groups, succeeded in arousing widespread popular opposition to the war.

It is interesting to observe similar phenomena in other countries, such as the US. There, two mass movements arose in the 1960's, one against the war in Vietnam and the other – the Civil Rights Movement - against racist laws in the southern states. And in the 1980s we witnessed the growing strength of the European anti-nuclear movement.

One may well ask what happened in each of these cases to enable peace movements to become so much stronger than usual that they had a significant influence on the actions of their country's leaders.

Sadat's visit came as a stunning surprise for Israelis. After the trauma of the 1973 war, the leader of the most powerful Arab state arrives out of the blue and offers to make peace with Israel - over the heads of its leaders! Israeli propaganda had always told us that our hand is extended in peace but the Arab states reject it. Now, after such a courageous and clear statement by the principal leader of the Arab world, there was a growing sense that the prime minister at the time, Menachem Begin, was doing everything in his power to squander chances for peace for the sake of his Greater Israel ideology and fulfillment of his desire to annex the Sinai Peninsula.

Out of this came the Reserve Officers' Letter calling upon Begin to choose the path of peace. Thousands of IDF reservists signed the letter, which was the precursor to the founding of the Peace Now movement. Peace Now's demonstrations attracted numbers unprecedented in this country, propelling the Israeli government towards a peace treaty with Egypt. Peace Now made a point of being "moderate," as distinct from more radical peace groups. Unlike the radical peace groups, which emphasized their differences with the country's leadership and its policies, Peace Now was very careful not to distance itself too much from the consensus position of Israeli society, thereby preserving its ability to carry on a dialogue with the "mainstream."

The second occasion when the Israeli peace movement developed into a mass movement was during the 1982 Lebanon war. This was a war about which there was a widespread feeling that not only the people but even the government had been misled about it. It was a war for which the leadership had no clear and convincing explanation as to why the government was jeopardizing the lives of our soldiers in a political conflict that had no bearing on our security. The radical peace movement, and subsequently other ad hoc groups, began to build popular opposition to the war. We saw groups such as Soldiers Against Silence, who demonstrated against the war when on leave from the front. We saw Mothers Against Silence and Parents Against Silence demonstrating as well. And for the first time in the history of Israel's wars, a military refusal movement (*Yesh Gvul* - Hebrew for "There is a limit/border!") emerged during wartime; supporting soldiers who refused to serve.

Four weeks after the war broke out, Peace Now, too, joined in the opposition and organized mass demonstrations that united all of the groups that opposed that unnecessary war. This time, too, there was an obvious difference between the radical and moderate peace groups. The radical groups had opposed the war from day one. Peace Now, though, was afraid to criticize the war as long as soldiers were fighting at the front. Only after a month, when they saw that opposition to the war was growing, did Peace Now openly join the struggle.

One could say that in this instance, the government had broken its unwritten "contract of trust" with the country's citizens, whereby the government takes them seriously and would do nothing to jeopardize their safety unless absolutely necessary.

The Vietnam War transformed the American peace movement into a mass movement. There, too, the country's leaders had been unable to persuade its citizens that this was a just war in which they were obliged to risk their lives. There, too, the government had violated its "contract of trust" with its citizens.

This raises the question of why the Iraq and Afghanistan wars did not also lead to the successful transformation of the US peace movement into a mass movement. It should be remembered that during the Vietnam War, the US still had a universal draft, whereas when the other two wars broke out, service in the American army was already voluntary, its ranks filled primarily by members of marginalized sectors of the population, who do not normally take to the streets to demonstrate their opposition to government policies. During Vietnam, when the well established and more educated classes were compelled to provide their sons as cannon-fodder, many of them joined anti-war protests. Once service in the armed forces became voluntary, the peace movement had a hard time recruiting masses of participants for its protests against these two unnecessary wars.

The Civil Rights Movement led by Martin Luther King Jr, which struggled against discrimination against blacks in the southern states of the US, is a highly interesting case. I do not know to what degree it was influenced by the legacy of the American Civil War, which put an end to slavery. It seems to me, though, that its main impact was through its practice of nonviolence.

Most whites in the US of that time regarded the country's black citizens in a negative light – violent, criminal, dangerous, scary, etc. The nonviolent struggle drew an inverse picture. Time and again blacks were seen demonstrating nonviolently and suffering from the violence of whites. The world was suddenly stood on its head. The violent, dangerous criminals were now the whites attacking nonviolent blacks who posed no threat to anyone, while the police, for the most part, did nothing to bring the assailants to justice. This exposed the whites' aggression against blacks, not only in demonstrations but also in their own homes and elsewhere. I believe this is what turned their movement into a mass movement that succeeded in recruiting many whites in support of its demands: As soon as whites were freed from their ingrained fear of blacks, they could see the injustice and cruelty of the racist laws. Martin Luther King Jr, himself, was arrested and jailed many times for flouting these racist laws. But now the birthday of this serial "criminal" is a national holiday in the US, declared by none other than President Ronald Reagan – a right-wing president – precisely because King succeeded in preventing bloodshed in a struggle whose previous chapter had ended in such a bloody civil war.[7]

Another instance when the peace movement's welcome influence was felt was in the 1980s when the US, as part of the Cold War, decided to place nuclear-armed Pershing 2 and Cruise missiles in several European countries. These were missiles that the Soviet radar system would have difficulty detecting until an estimated 5-10 minutes before hitting their targets. In other words, there would not be time to confirm the accuracy of the radar system's report of a launch of ballistic missiles against the USSR. In the past, nuclear war had been narrowly averted thanks to the time lag between detection and impact. The new missiles, therefore, increased the chance of a nuclear war breaking out as the result of a detection error. The peace movement in Europe, in working to prevent the deployment of these missiles, swelled to a mass movement. Here again, the governments were seen as violating their citizens' trust. Indeed, a few years later, these missiles were removed from Europe in the context of the Intermediate-Range Nuclear Forces Treaty between the US and Russia.

---

7   See also: Learning from Martin Luther King Jr.'s successful non-violent struggle p.166

LEARNING FROM THE SUCCESS OF THE CIVIL RIGHTS MOVEMENT IN THE US

As with the blacks in the US – who were perceived by most whites as dangerous - so too, in our case, the Palestinians are perceived by Israelis and most of the Western World as dangerous rather than as victims. The occupier/oppressor always perceives his victims as dangerous; how else would he justify his own deeds to himself? It seems to me that only a Palestinian struggle of a nonviolent nature, like that of the blacks in the US civil rights movement, will liberate Israelis from their fear of annihilation, while also having an influence on the Western World – Israel's principal source of backing and support. This kind of struggle would also serve to level the playing field in the continuing conflict over this country. After all, Israel obviously has a huge advantage over the Palestinians in violent conflict. By contrast, a fully nonviolent struggle would both free Israelis from their anxiety over security and enable many of them to see the horrific injustice of Israel's actions towards the Palestinians. Thus, a struggle of this nature would create a rift between the majority of Israelis concerned about their safety and the government of Israel, which prioritizes territorial expansion over the security of its citizens. Such a struggle would also have a greater influence on supporters of Israel worldwide. Indeed, with the recent drop in the level of Palestinian violence, we are seeing the BDS (Boycott, Divestment and Sanctions) movement (which calls for an economic, cultural, and academic boycott of Israel because of the continuing occupation) growing stronger.

As long as suicide bombers were blowing themselves up in the streets of Israel's cities, the BDS movement had no chance of increasing its power and influence. A total halt to Palestinian violence would reinforce and speed up the growth of this movement's influence on the nations of the West. It is, by the way, important to note that the BDS movement brings pressure to bear not only on Israel but on the Palestinians as well. Only when the level of their violence is low do the Palestinians succeed in reaching increasingly broad audiences throughout the world. Should Palestinian violence increase, many supporters would abandon BDS. We should also note that, in the case of boycott, as in any nonviolent campaign, the target can put an end to it at any time; i.e., as soon as Israel announces an end to the occupation and agrees to a Palestinian state by its side, I believe that most supporters of BDS will abandon the struggle, despite the fact that the other two demands of the campaign (as laid out at https://bdsmovement.net/what-is-bds) have not been met.

Violent struggle derives its strength from each side's fear that its security and survival is threatened by its opponent. Nonviolent struggle's strength derives from one's opponent's liberation from fear for their security and their very existence. In other words, when we choose nonviolence, we are not seeking to threaten the existence of the other, but are simply demanding justice. Several years ago, rumor had it that Hamas was planning to send 100,000 refugees from Gaza towards their homes and villages inside Israel, which had been destroyed in 1948. This action was supposed to be carried out purely nonviolently. Israel was seriously frightened at the prospect.

How could the nonviolent march be prevented without terrible damage to Israel's image and status in the world? "Luckily" for Israel, Hamas did not carry out this action - for one simple reason: choosing nonviolence requires giving up the goal of wiping out the other side, and struggling instead to obtain justice for one's own side.

Another difference between violence and nonviolence is evident in the fact that, while the former is based on mistrust of the other side, the latter attempts to build mutual trust and to move from a "balance of fear" to a "balance of trust."

Nonviolent Palestinian struggle actually heightens the security of Israel's citizens. It is a struggle that would not cost Israeli lives, whether of civilians, soldiers, or settlers. And it is a struggle that would expose the truth about the conflict: that for the government of Israel, territorial expansion is far more important than bolstering the security of its citizens.

AN ESCALATION OF NONVIOLENCE

It is very easy for me, as an Israeli, to preach nonviolence to Palestinians, but it seems to me that, if we truly desire to achieve peace and to avoid war and its casualties, we Israelis must also make the transition from violence to nonviolence.

As Israeli citizens, it is in our interest for the struggle to move from the path of violence to that of nonviolence. Here I would like to introduce a concept that I call "an escalation of nonviolence." In general, conflicts escalate from disagreement, through increasing levels of mutual anger, on to physical attacks - where every injury provokes the other side to seek revenge and justifies a violent response – and right up to full-scale war. I propose to move in the opposite direction: an escalation of nonviolence, whereby the flames of war would be dampened in response to nonviolent actions, moving the adversaries away from a state of war. This would reduce the level of violence by the other side and so on until violence ceased on both sides and peace was achieved - since as soon as one side refrains from violence, the other side loses its justification for using violence. When the level of violence is reduced, the urge for revenge diminishes as well. As violence decreases, so does anxiety about security. All of these steps facilitate a transition to negotiations and to the compromises necessary for the achievement of peace.

There are nonviolent options available to all parties in a conflict. For these I propose the following four categories:

1. Active nonviolence;
2. Preventive nonviolence;
3. Nonviolence by a third party that is not aligned with either side in the conflict;
4. Nonviolence that enables cooperation amongst all sides in the conflict.

Active nonviolence is, in essence, the form of nonviolent struggle available to the Palestinians. Historical examples include India's struggle for independence against British rule, led by Mahatma Gandhi, and the struggle of blacks in the US against the racist laws of the southern states, led by Dr. Martin Luther King Jr.

During the First Intifada, the Palestinians employed numerous nonviolent tactics: strikes, demonstrations, declarations of independence by villages, boycott of Israeli goods (and growing food to replace Israeli produce), determining for themselves when the shops would open and close, and refusal to pay taxes imposed by Israel. Nonetheless, frequent stone throwing made it easy for Israel to present the struggle as a violent one requiring a response by the Israeli army. In its propaganda, Israel used the stone throwing as justification for its suppression of the Palestinian uprising, frequently stating that "stones can kill." Even so, the level of Israeli army violence during the First Intifada was lower than during the Second, when Palestinians, too, waged an armed struggle.

Palestinian nonviolent initiatives are not a recent phenomenon. Another example from the 1980s was the PLO's "Ship of Return." The idea was to sail into Haifa harbor carrying Palestinian refugees homeward, accompanied by representatives of a variety of international media and solidarity organizations, as well as some internationally known figures. Israel sabotaged the ship in the Cypriot port of Limassol where it was awaiting these passengers' arrival from Athens.

In 2011, when Israeli soldiers began forcing Palestinian school children to go through metal detectors on their way to school on Shuhada Street in Hebron, the teachers and students responded by holding their classes at the side of the road, before the checkpoint. On the third day, Israeli soldiers fired teargas canisters at the teachers and children. Now the children go through the metal detector on their way to and from school. Teargas is more of a health hazard than the metal detector.

There are, of course, numerous other nonviolent tactics, many of which are already being employed by Palestinians and many others that could be. The former include the March of Return, *Sumud* (steadfastly clinging to their land and homes), the replanting of orchards uprooted by Israeli military or settlers, the reconstruction of houses demolished by Israel, etc.

Preventive nonviolence is the mode of nonviolent action most often employed by Israelis. Historically, this was employed by the Quakers who settled Pennsylvania in the 17th century. William Penn, a Quaker, received the territory from the English crown. Many Quakers immigrated to America because of religious persecution in England. Recognizing that the land they were moving to belonged to those who already lived on it and not to the British crown, they held negotiations with the indigenous population regarding permission to settle there. In addition, they purchased every plot of land they wished to settle from the indigenous inhabitants. The Quakers refrained from setting up a military force, and the Great

Treaty between them and the local Indian chiefs in the early 1680s remained unbroken for some 70 years (in contrast to the state of affairs in New England, where Puritans desecrated Indian burial grounds, hunted down and scalped Indians, and sold indigenous women and children into slavery). Eventually non-Quaker settlers came to outnumber the Quakers in Pennsylvania. Many of these rejected Quaker ways, abandoning the path of peace; and Pennsylvania, too, saw wars between whites and the indigenous population.

One might say that most or all of the demands that the Israeli peace movement has made of the government are in the realm of preventive nonviolence. When we demand that the government cease its land grabs, home demolitions, expulsions, building of settlements, theft of water and other resources and, most importantly, that it put an end to the occupation, we are demanding an end to actions that are made possible only by the use of military force and which, in turn, give rise to Palestinian acts of revenge.

The question remains, what can we do in the realm of preventive nonviolence when the government does not accede to our demands? When conscientious objectors (both ours and others') refuse to serve as military tools of the ruling power, they are in fact carrying out an act of preventive nonviolence. Similarly, those who refuse to serve in the Occupied Territories, even though willing to serve elsewhere, are performing an act of preventive nonviolence. Israelis who boycott settlement products do so as well, as do Israelis who refuse to work in the settlements or otherwise in support of the occupation. These are actions that challenge the legitimacy of an occupation that, by its very nature, is dependent upon the violence exerted by the Israeli army which, in turn, provokes violence on the part of Palestinians resisting the occupation and their expulsion from their land, homes, and country.

A third side that is not aligned with either party to the conflict can work for its resolution or at least for the cessation of hostilities by both sides. On the most basic level, we see this in quarrels among children. When two children are hitting each other, a third child might intervene in an attempt to stop the fight. He can do so only if neither of the adversaries regard him as an enemy, so they won't hurt him. Of course, other children also might actually intensify the conflict and the violence it entails. On the political level, we see UN forces sent to serve as a buffer between warring sides in order to maintain a ceasefire between them. The UN can do this by virtue of its role as a "third side" that is not the enemy of either party to the conflict. Originally, by the way, UN peace-keeping forces were unarmed. States, too, can mediate conflicts between other countries when they enter the scene as a "third side." An example is the US role as mediator in the peace negotiations between Israel and Egypt. Here too, as in the schoolyard, states often may contribute to a conflict, for example, by selling weapons to any of the parties involved.

Of course it is also possible to intervene as an third party using a nonviolent approach. We see this in our own conflict, when peace and human rights activists from countries that are not party to the conflict come and intervene nonviolently in an effort to reduce harm and lower the level of violence. An example is the Christian Peacemaker Team (CPT) that has been active in Hebron since the mid-1990s, endeavoring to nonviolently protect Palestinians from attacks by settlers and soldiers in Hebron itself and in the South Hebron Hills. And during the period of frequent Palestinian attacks on Israeli buses, CPT volunteers would ride the bus lines where most of the attacks took place. They have also intervened on many occasions when Palestinians were throwing stones at soldiers or settlers, with the goal of stopping the stone-throwing. All this is done nonviolently, by virtue of their status as a nonaligned third party.

Since the outbreak of the Second Intifada, additional organizations - both Israeli and International - have been active in the West Bank and Gaza Strip, employing nonviolent tactics to protect Palestinians who are being attacked by settlers and soldiers.

Nonviolence makes it possible for activists from both "sides" to work together: Israeli peace and human rights activists participate in the Palestinian olive harvest or in planting olive trees in places where soldiers or settlers have uprooted them, and in the reconstruction of Palestinian homes demolished by the Israeli army. This kind of activism can also find expression in joint demonstrations. Even those Israelis who regard the Palestinian position as just are not willing to participate in a violent struggle against their own people. But when the struggle employs nonviolent tactics, they can join in action for justice, peace, and human rights side-by-side with the Palestinians. In such joint actions, if soldiers or settlers show up, the Israeli activists function as the third party, and often succeed in lowering the level of violence significantly.

In all actions of this sort, we also see internationals alongside the Palestinian and Israeli activists; i.e., when actions are not violent, activists from all three "sides" of the conflict are able to cooperate. It is in this context that we must view the cooperation with Palestinians on the part of the international community that that is made possible by the employment of nonviolence. The Palestinian-initiated international BDS movement has succeeded in mobilizing an ever-increasing number of supporters, thanks to the concurrent reduction in the level of Palestinian violence. As long as bombs were going off in buses or restaurants in Israeli cities, there was little or no chance that many outside observers would be willing or able to see these as the acts of Palestinians driven to desperation by an oppressive Israeli military occupation that denies them their most basic rights. Only when terrorist attacks cease is there any chance that more and more people will be able to discern who is the occupier and who the occupied, who the attacker and who the victim. Unlike in the case of the Ship of Return and that of the children and their teachers in Hebron, military force will not be of use in squelching the BDS campaign. Although it is true that pro-Israel Jewish and Christian Zionist (!) organizations try hard to put down this nonviolent struggle, they will not be able to achieve this by force of arms.

What I am advocating here is the launching of a process of "escalation of nonviolence," whereby nonviolent action by each side would reduce the other side's fear of its opposite number and would dissipate their mutual mistrust, thereby enabling reduction in the level of violence until its complete cessation and paving the way for a peace treaty. In order to achieve this, more and more people on both sides would need to be encouraged to abandon violence and adopt nonviolence.

On the Israeli right and in government circles, there is much anger towards those Israelis who practice preventive nonviolence. But these activists, by promoting an escalation of nonviolence, are actually enhancing the security of their Israeli compatriots. The more Palestinians turn to nonviolence, the safer Israelis will be. One cannot repudiate the violence of one's adversaries (especially while using violence against them) and not offer alternative methods of struggle; i.e., nonviolence. If we in the Israeli peace movement are to increase our influence within Israeli society, it will be by utilizing nonviolence to reduce the violence of Palestinian resistance to the occupation. In this way, we shall make it evident to our fellow citizens that their security is not the reason for the occupation and for the intransigence of Israel's governments past and present in resisting efforts to bring about peace. I believe that nonviolence will reduce security-related anxiety and strengthen the Israeli peace movement, to the point where sufficient pressure can be exerted to bring about an end to the occupation and the achievement of the peace we all hope for.

NONVIOLENCE AS A WAY TO PREVENT CIVIL WAR

Nonviolence is supposed to be the way to struggle against the occupation so as to bring about both its end and the achievement of peace between the two peoples. Amongst Israelis, the greatest fear is that an end to the occupation would lead to conflict between the zealot and existential Zionists, culminating in civil war. And the question is whether we have nonviolent methods for preventing – or reducing the threat of - a violent confrontation between these two sides.

Israel's policy of territorial expansionism has resulted in the extreme polarization of the country's society. The aspirations for peace held by one portion of the population are on a collision course with the religious settlers' belief in a divine promise of a "Greater Israel." What would constitute fulfillment of the wishes of one section of the population would be perceived as disastrous by the other. This is a situation requiring great care on the part of the government in order to forestall the explosion that such a change in policy is liable to ignite. Meanwhile it is important to bear in mind that the evacuation of the Gaza settlements during the "disengagement" of 2005 was carried out without significant violence by either side (Interestingly, there were two people offered nonviolence training to both the army and the settlers).

Most instances of nonviolent struggle that we know about are those waged by the oppressed against their oppressors. Here, however, we need to consider nonviolent means to be employed by government forces to deal with opposition from within. Of course a government has access to different means than do its opponents. It can pass laws; it can set policy. And a government is used to having in its hands the power to impose its policies; i.e., the military and police. What I propose is a nonviolent way for the government to impose its will, in hopes that this will prevent the civil war we all fear.

I think it is important to mention here the dispute between the leftist soldiers who refuse to serve in the Occupied Territories and their opponents. Many argue that these refuseniks are lending legitimacy to refusal to serve by right-wingers (e.g., those who refuse to participate in the eviction of settlers), and indeed, refusal to serve does make it more difficult for the government to implement its policies. I am sorry to say that Yitzhak Rabin's assassination and the threats against Ariel Sharon's life have shown us just how far the Zionist zealots are liable to go should the Israeli government change course and adopt a peace policy. Thus, above and beyond the struggle between left and right over policy, there is also a dispute over what means of struggle are legitimate in the intra-Israeli context. The left-wing military refusers do set such boundaries: You receive an order against which your whole being rebels? Then lay down your weapon and refuse! Do not take up arms against the government whose policy outrages you. That is the limit!

I hope that, if we reach the point where the government of Israel does move towards peace, the soldiers from the zealot-like right will refuse to carry out orders but will not take up arms against the state and its government, just as the leftist refusniks do! This would be their nonviolent struggle against a policy that they oppose to their very core.

In our case, the government has at its disposal several courses of action that are not violent. It could, for example, decide that Israel abide by the 2004 advisory opinion of the International Court of Justice in the Hague, which stated, *inter alia*, that the Fourth Geneva Convention applies to the West Bank. This means that all of the settlements there are illegal, and accepting this would require that Israel return all of the land that settlers have forcibly taken over and, likewise, all of the restrictive military orders that have been imposed upon the civilian population under occupation would need to be reversed. The return of the majority of the stolen land to its Palestinian owners would be the first step. The theft of water and mineral resources would also need to stop. Government subsidization of the settlement project would come to an end; the government could stop designating the settlements as priority development areas, and restore that designation to communities on Israel's periphery, as was the case originally.

The government could also institute a policy of encouraging settlers to return to Israel proper. It could pass laws compensating the returnees so that the move would not hurt them financially, with the amount of compensation contingent on their not damaging the property left behind (I am assuming that, as a part of a peace treaty, the settlement buildings could constitute a portion of the reparations paid to Palestinian refugees). Instead of forcibly evacuating the settlements, the government could set a date when municipal services would be cut off and the army would cease to provide protection. And, just as exchanges of territory between Israel and Palestine would be part of a peace treaty, so the most settlers could remain where they are, such an arrangement (for settlements that are in the parts that will be Palestine) could stipulate that most settlers could remain where they are, on the understanding that for each settler who remained on Palestinian soil, a Palestinian refugee would be admitted into Israel. This would make it attractive to the Palestinians to accept those settlers who wished to remain as Palestinian citizens. It would also serve as an incentive for those settlers who don't wish to live under Palestinian jurisdiction to return to Israel proper.

LEARNING FROM THE END OF THE FRENCH OCCUPATION OF ALGERIA

In reaction to the decision by President De Gaulle and the government of France to withdraw from Algeria and to end the French occupation of that country, initially both settlers and army generals opposed to the withdrawal rebelled. The French solved the problem of getting the settlers to leave Algeria by informing them that the army would depart on a certain date, leaving them to their own devices.

The French had no messianic religious sentiments regarding Algeria, so it was relatively easy for them give it up. With us, the chief difficulty lies with the Zionist zealots, whose political agenda is enmeshed in their messianic-religious faith, rendering them averse to compromise. They attempt to impose their perspective on all of us, and I fear that they might go so far as to threaten civil war in their resistance to a peace that would require withdrawal from the West Bank. It's important to remember that despite their being a small minority within Israeli society, they are extremely determined in fighting for their beliefs. Unlike most of the left, who have abandoned their sense of commitment and have come to embody blatant hedonism, these zealots have remained highly dedicated to their beliefs. Therefore, they have far more power than their relative proportion in Israeli society. They also have installed their people throughout the Israeli civil service, which would make it very difficult for politicians to implement their decisions, should these be contrary to the views and objectives of Zionist zealots in public service positions.

It seems to me that the French example is more relevant to an Israeli withdrawal from the Golan Heights, where security is the main justification for continuation of Israeli rule. We must recall that most of the settlers in the Golan come from the "existential" branch of Zionism, and that their motivation for settling there was based more on security concerns than on a divine promise or attachment to the landscape of our ancient homeland. In the event that we arrive at an agreement with Syria that leads to peace (if that country survives its current civil war in one piece), these settlers would initially vehemently oppose the new state of affairs, but would eventually come to terms with it.

From the above, we can understand the purpose for which settlements were established from the very start; i.e., it is much more difficult to dismantle civilian settlements than military bases (remember the evacuation of the Israeli army bases in South Lebanon in comparison with that of the Gaza Strip settlements). It is true that the Golan settlers enjoy broad-based public support, not based on religious sentiments, but stemming from anxieties regarding security. Therefore, if a peace treaty with Syria were to address Israeli security concerns, it would be far easier to evacuate the Golan.

THE DEBATE WITHIN THE PEACE MOVEMENT

The radical peace movement in Israel today is split by the debate between supporters of the two-state solution to the Israeli-Palestinian conflict and those who advocate a one-state solution. Personally I stand with those who support the two-state solution. Let me explain my position:

If the conflict is understood as a historical process whereby one group has invaded the living space of another, forcing the original inhabitants out of the territory, then it is obvious that hostilities between the groups will continue until this process stops. This is, after all, the essence of the conflict. I believe that only a two-state solution can place limits on the Zionist appetite for expansion, thereby fulfilling the primary condition for peace between the two peoples. That is why I support the Geneva Initiative of 2003, when Palestinians and Israelis sat together and carried on alternative peace negotiations based upon the compromises proposed by the then US President, Bill Clinton, following the failed Camp David talks of 2000. Fundamental to the Geneva Accord is the fixing of borders between Israel and the West Bank and between Israel and the Gaza Strip ("Between the states of Palestine and Israel") "in accordance with UN Security Council Resolutions 242 and 338" based on the pre-1967 War lines "with reciprocal modifications on a 1:1 basis" (http://www.geneva-accord.org), such that most settlers would remain where they are, and these areas would be annexed to Israel. In exchange, Israel would transfer an equal amount of its land to the *Palestinian st*ate.

The Arab League's proposal of 2002 is based upon the same criterion – return of occupied territory in exchange for peace. In other words, as soon as Israel formally accepts as its borders the armistice lines of 1949, as do all countries that have recognized Israel, it will be able to achieve peace with the Palestinians and the rest of the Arab and Muslim world. After all, that is what happened following Israel's peace treaty with Egypt in 1979, once Israel had returned the Sinai Peninsula, which it had captured in 1967, to Egypt. Incidentally, the only borders of Israel that are recognized by international law are those that were the laid out in the peace treaties between Israel and Egypt and Jordan, respectively.

There was a time when I believed that it was beneficial that the one-state solution was being proposed. I thought that the threat to the maintenance of a Jewish majority presented by a single state would serve to pressure the Israeli government to call a halt to its undeclared policy of annexing occupied territory. However, the results of the Oslo process created a new situation in which the idea of one state was no longer relevant as a means for pressuring Israel. Today, even leaders of the Zionist zealots accept the reality created by the Oslo process as a feasible solution, and speak of annexing Area C of the West Bank, while leaving Palestinian "Bantustans" in Areas A and B. This has also been the unofficial policy of Israeli governments, past and present. Looking at the distribution of house demolitions, destruction of villages and cisterns, at road blocks and all the other restrictions imposed upon Palestinians in Area C, one clearly understands that what we have here is an ongoing attempt to cause as many Palestinians as possible to leave Area C and move to Areas A and B. This is the strategy that the Israeli government, finding itself enmeshed in a thicket of international constraints, came up with for dealing with the "demographic threat" posed by an increased Palestinian population: annexation of more territory without increasing the number of Palestinians and the demographic peril this would pose to Israel's maintenance of a Jewish majority.

If we move towards a solution where both peoples share a single state, we shall have a situation where the Jews are in the "first world" and the Palestinians are, by and large, in the "third world." The economic disparities between these national/ religious sectors would result in the continuation of the conflict within the single state. The Jews, thanks to their economic advantage, would continue to purchase land from the Palestinians, so that the process of pushing Palestinians out of the country would not cease. After all, as stated above, this is the core issue of the conflict: one society invading the living space of another and forcing out the original inhabitants.

The one-state solution sounds ideal. What could be nobler than the two peoples in conflict over the land overcoming past grievances and moving forward to a shared life of peace and reconciliation? The problem is that in order to achieve such a wonderful solution, a profound change of heart is required, one giving rise to a sense of common humanity that transcends the divides of nationality and religion. Without this profound change, the conflict would simply go from being a state of war between occupier and occupied to a conflict between two societies within the same state.

By contrast, the vision of two states must be built upon and expanded. We should aspire to a European Union-like process of evolving into a common market of the entire Middle East, in hopes of this eventually leading to a process of Middle East unification. Even after centuries of ceaseless warfare, Europe embarked upon a process of unification that rendered borders and national differences unimportant. They were following the example of the Swiss who, many years earlier, had overcome their internal national differences to form a federation, living peacefully amongst themselves and with the rest of the world for a very long time. If the Europeans were to continue in this direction, we might even end up seeing a "United States of Europe." I very much wish that we, too, will be wise enough to follow this path as a buttress for peace and a way to ensure our survival.

Sadly, my comrades in the peace movement who favor the one-state solution have, themselves, become irrelevant, having essentially given in to the annexation policy promoted by Israeli right-wingers and put into practice by the government. Now, when support for a two-state solution has become increasingly widespread outside of Israel, they stand aside and, as a result, the Israeli peace movement is weakened. What a waste.

THE CLASH BETWEEN LAW AND MORALITY JEOPARDIZES ISRAEL'S SURVIVAL

A final word of caution. There have been at least three other instances in modern history that I can recall, where the laws of a country have clashed openly and blatantly with moral values: Nazi Germany's Nuremberg Laws, the racist/segregationist ("Jim Crow") laws of the US South, and the apartheid laws of South Africa. In all of these cases, campaigns against these laws eventually brought about their abolition. In Germany and South Africa, an additional result was a profound alteration in the form of government.

A country's laws play a very important role in ensuring that all of its citizens and resident aliens can conduct their lives in a manner conducive to the greater good of all. When laws are passed that are harmful to a portion of the citizenry on account of ethnic, religious, racial, gender, or other differences, a situation is created wherein it is justifiable to oppose or even to violate these laws. Criminal law, at least, is supposed to prevent immoral acts. When laws are in conflict with morality, their existence is no longer justified, and it is our duty oppose them and the policies they were created to serve.

Laws and policies of this kind are turning Israel into a pariah state. As the Israeli-Palestinian conflict continues, and with it an ongoing policy of forcing Palestinians out of the Occupied Territories and of discrimination against the Palestinian citizens of Israel – especially injurious to Israel's Bedouin population – it becomes obvious that laws promoting theft and discrimination are at odds with morality. It is because of this that Israel's international backing has been diminishing and, sooner or later, even within Israel itself, the number opposing these discriminatory and hurtful laws and the racist and nationalistic application of neutral laws will grow. Eventually, the reality of the situation will become obvious to all, and everyone will see through the attempted obfuscation, through the use of "universal" language, of the racist and nationalistic intent of these laws and their application. If we want Israel to continue to exist in this region, we must put an end to its expansionist policies and move towards peace agreements with our neighbors, agreements that would guarantee Israel's survival.

PART 4

ADDITIONAL ARTICLES: TRY TO UNDERSTAND BETTER

THE ETHICAL PROBLEM

War brings us face-to-face with contradictions between our sense of morality and the perception that we need to protect ourselves from enemies who are endangering our lives. Armies are established to defend against external enemies that threaten lives and security, and police forces are set up to protect society from internal enemies (criminals). What is at work here is a mechanism for the legitimization of acts contrary to morality in the name of safeguarding moral values such as the preservation of life, the protection of property and way of life, and the prevention of suffering. In the name of safeguarding these values, we are legitimizing acts that, in and of themselves, are immoral, such as the utilization of violence and killing. We therefore grant to armies and the police the exclusive right to employ lethal force - in itself immoral - in order to prevent the wanton exercise of violence.

So, a young recruit comes to the army after years of having been inculcated with moral values, both formally and informally. He now must learn how most effectively to carry out acts that are contrary to morality. He learns that he must obey orders. His moral judgment is undermined. He no longer is allowed to exercise moral judgment: "Now you just follow orders. Now morality and law are in the hands of the army and your commanding officers." And often, when a soldier acts violently, killing and performing other acts that are contrary to both morality and criminal law, he is considered a hero and at times is even decorated for his actions.

The contradictions between morality and the demands of war requires an especially strong ethical code, otherwise, it is but a slippery slope from a military/policing ethos to that of a criminal organization that violates moral principles to reach its objectives. Strict adherence to rigorous ethical standards is the only way to maintain the distinction between the military and police, on the one hand, and a criminal organization, on the other.

In differentiating between ethics and morality in this context, I propose the following distinction: morality in essence deals with the protection of life, ways of life, and with the prevention of suffering; whereas ethics basically provides principles for fair conduct in social systems and their interpersonal relations. Every profession and professional organization has its own ethical rules. In short, morality provides a code of conduct for individuals, whereas ethics provide such a code for professions and trades and their associated organizations. A code of ethics is essentially a moral code specific to a given trade or profession.

In order for people to be able to practice any trade or profession, it is an ethical requirement that they must undergo a period of training to become qualified in that trade or profession, so that their usefulness will be greater than the risk that they might cause harm. Physicians who haven't properly learned their profession will harm their patients; likewise lawyers or construction workers, and so on. The code of ethics of each profession or trade also defines the boundaries of its behavior. For example, physicians must obtain permission from patients before performing certain procedures, as must lawyers.

In the case of soldiers, on the other hand, the principle of fair conduct is not dependent on the agreement of the other side. They must therefore be even more careful to conduct themselves ethically than members of other professions. Military ethics require that soldiers not employ force against those who are unable to defend themselves. This means that defenseless civilians should not be attacked, and if an opponent surrenders or is wounded and thereby "neutralized," the fighting must cease.

Here I want to write about three ethical principles that seem to me to be especially important. The first of these is that the military and police are meant to protect us from those who would harm us or threaten our lives and security. As soon as the military and police are involved in such actions as the dispossession of another people, they are acting in contravention to the ethics of war, armies, and police forces. Of course, when the army and police rescue victims of a natural disaster, they are fulfilling their role in accordance with these ethics, the "enemy", in this case, being the forces of nature that endanger lives.

The second and most fundamental ethical principle is fairness; i.e., differentiating between combatants and civilians. This means that a soldier fights a soldier, a fellow combatant, and never a defenseless civilian. After all, breaking in to the homes or businesses of defenseless citizens to rob them or steal their property is exactly what criminal organizations do. They do not rob those who first robbed them, but rather random citizens or those who, in their opinion, possess great or excessive wealth. Anyone who stands in their way risks injury or death. And of course police, when fighting crime or responding to disturbances of the peace, must refrain from killing people who don't constitute a threat to their lives.

The third principle has to do with the question of "Who started it?" In order for there to be justification for the use of means that are intrinsically immoral, we need to ask, "What did one side in the conflict do to justify the violent response of the other side?" When Israel fought the Arab armies in the June 1967 War, it was operating within the framework of the ethics of war: an army fighting other armies. Israel launched its attack on the Egyptian air force bases in the wake of Egypt's violation of the conditions surrounding the demilitarized status of the Sinai Peninsula and its threatened maritime blockade of the Straits of Tiran. There was also a threat of invasion by the armies of Egypt, Jordan, and Syria.

After the imposition of the occupation, the Israeli army was left facing a defenseless civilian population. The people of the occupied territories were supposed to be protected by the military ethic, which states that soldiers fight soldiers and not defenseless civilians. It does not permit actions liable to harm the population under occupation unless clearly necessitated by security concerns. Just as criminal law imparts legal power to moral principles, so too, international law (e.g., the Hague and Geneva conventions) is meant to grant protection to a population under occupation in accordance with the ethics of war; i.e., by placing limits on the actions of the military vis a vis civilian members of that population. As soon as Israel decided that on certain issues its army would not abide by the principles of military ethics and international conventions regarding the conduct of war, it risked turning its own army into a criminal organization.

The ethical problem is intensified when dealing with terrorist organizations that conduct their activities while in the midst of the civilian population. According to the ethics of war, if someone attacks you, you are entitled to retaliate. But if he launches his attack while hidden amongst noncombatants, he is endangering them, whether or not they are willing, by compelling their involvement (albeit passive) in his hostile acts – something that military ethics attempts to avoid. This is where "proportionality" enters the picture. How much force may be employed against terrorists hiding amongst civilians, so as to minimize injuries to the noncombatants? And how much effort is to be made to avoid harming the latter? Proportionality is an important criterion, but inexact and thus quite problematic. By the way, if terrorists who plan to attack Israel attempted to establish their bases in open areas, away from civilian population centers, the Israeli army would wipe them out immediately. So if they choose to employ violence against us, they have no choice but to operate from civilian areas. Incidentally, this is exactly what the Jewish undergrounds did, too, during their struggle against British Mandatory rule in pre-state Palestine.

Here we must ask ourselves why the State of Israel maintains a number of its own military bases inside major cities. After all, it is a nation state, and no one is preventing it from establishing army bases outside of civilian population centers. By having military bases inside cities, Israel is legitimizing attacks by its enemies against those very cities.

The ethical issue is much clearer and more serious in the unilateral war that the Israeli army is waging against the Palestinian civilian population in the Occupied Territories. Theft of land, demolition of houses, expulsion from home and land, the establishment of Jewish settlements, and the theft of water and other resources are the most important component in the IDF's unilateral war against defenseless Palestinian civilians – in the process of "inheriting the land." These are not acts of self-defense, and none of them have anything to do with security. These are actions whose sole purpose is the transfer of the country from the Palestinians to the State of Israel. In this, the Israeli army is acting like a criminal organization, using force to appropriate property (i.e., land) coveted by the state. Neither the plethora of military orders arbitrarily imposed by the IDF in the Occupied Territories nor any of Israel's legislative manipulations are of any help in rendering "kosher" the theft of land from defenseless Palestinians living under Israeli occupation. All they accomplish is the criminalization of the Israeli legal system – putting it both at odds with morality and in violation of international law (from which the ethics of war derive their legal basis).

The situation is similar for those citizens of Israel who have the misfortune of having been born Palestinian in the "Jewish state." Here too, with the help of legislation, legal manipulations, and the use of military and policing force, the state has transferred most of their landholdings into its own hands and has defined most of their construction initiatives as illegal. Again, through discriminatory laws and the racist-nationalistic implementation of neutral laws, Israel discriminates against its own Palestinian citizens and causes them injury. In their case, as in the West Bank, Israel has passed legislation that violates international human rights conventions intended to protect people from the whims of arbitrary rule. And here, too, on most occasions when the police confiscate land, demolish homes, or destroy crops, they are acting in contravention to police ethics; instead of a body dedicated to fighting crime, they themselves become a criminal organization. And here, we mustn't forget the "Yoav Unit" of the Israeli police, created especially to perpetrate the state's crimes against the Bedouin living in the Negev.

Israel endeavors to avoid fatalities when expelling Palestinians from their homes and land. This minimizes media interest in the doings of Israel's "security" forces and perpetuates the illusion that the IDF is a "moral army." Going back to the example of criminal organizations, one should remember that they, too, carry out their activities largely without the taking of lives. But just as criminals say to their victims, "Your property or your life"... so does the Israeli army demand – (Palestinian) property, or else - life.

This is where the ethical dilemma facing Palestinians begins. How are they supposed to protect their lives and property, including their homes, land, and natural resources? After most of them have already been expelled from their farmland, homes, and territory, along comes an occupation army and uses its might and its laws to take almost all that remains. How can they defend themselves against those who are methodically forcing them out? After all, they cannot mount an army, since Israel would immediately annihilate it. The Palestinian police force created under Israel's auspices is restricted to the internal policing of Palestinian society, and is not permitted to intervene and put an end to the ongoing theft of Palestinian property. From the perspective of ethics of war, they are fully justified in fighting against those who are pushing them out of their homeland. Some Palestinians, then, have resorted to terrorism. Naturally this cannot prevent the theft of their land or do away with the threat to Palestinian lives, so it takes the form of retaliatory attacks. This is where the ethical problem comes in. When they attack a military target, they are operating in accordance with the ethics of war. When they take action against (Israeli) civilians, this contravenes the ethics of war. And when they hide amongst civilians, they legitimize – even if to a limited extent – Israeli attacks on the very civilians on whose behalf they ostensibly are fighting. The justice of their cause is not relevant to this ethical dilemma. Even if your struggle is totally justified (and everyone believes their cause is just), you must act in accordance with the ethics of war.

UTILIZING THE LEGAL SYSTEM

We often think about a country's legal system in the terms of criminal law, which provides a legal basis for the moral strictures on our conduct: it is forbidden to murder, kill, rob, steal, rape, commit assault, etc. These are legal prohibitions against immoral acts. My point here is that legal systems also include laws that have no direct moral significance, nor do they define norms. Instead, they constitute secondary legislation, setting parameters for what behavior is permitted in a variety of areas, such as driving, work, the economy, marital status, personal property and real estate, planning and construction, etc. In these areas, the function of the many branches of formal-procedural legislation is to regulate day-to-day life, and most of this has no moral significance in and of itself.

Thus, side-by-side with legislation that serves the interests of Israel's power brokers - promulgated to further their world views and ideologies - Israeli citizens conduct their lives on the basis of obedience to regulations and procedures that constitute the general normative framework of the society, but which are themselves without moral significance. After all, it makes no difference if people in one country drive on the right side of the road, whereas in another they drive on the left. The important thing is simply that all drivers in the same country obey the same set of laws in order to prevent chaos.

Regarding the matter at hand, I shall focus on legislation regarding land ownership and planning and construction. These laws are expressions of government policy and of Israel's aspirations regarding the shaping of the geographic and demographic space. One of the principal ways this plays out is in the implementation of Zionist policies of control of the country. In fact, prior to the founding of the state, only 7- 8% of the land was in Jewish hands, whereas today that figure is 96%. This massive transfer of land from Palestinian to Jewish possession has only been possible because of the legislation passed for this very purpose.

THE CLASH BETWEEN LAW AND MORALITY

In this realm, one can see many instances of legislation at odds with moral values. Imagine that the Knesset was asked to include a law legalizing robbery in the country's Criminal Code. I am sure that every Member of Knesset would reject such an outrageous proposal and would refuse to pass such a law on the grounds of its immorality. Yet the very same Knesset that would rebel against such a request has passed a whole string of laws regulating the acquisition and ownership of land that amount to a land grab. One example is the Land Acquisition (Validity of Acts and Compensation) Law of 1953. Utilizing this law, Israel has transferred to itself land belonging to Bedouin and other Palestinian citizens after evicting them on various pretexts - such as army maneuvers in their area which require them to be evacuated "for their own safety" for "six months" - and never allowing them to return. Their "abandoned" land, however, is taken over by the state through the enforcement of the abovementioned law.

Another example of a law that Israel has used for the take-over of Palestinians' land is the Absentee Property Law of 1950.

Even Palestinians who remained inside the borders of what became Israel after fleeing their homes during the hostilities of the 1948 War were prohibited by this law from returning to their land and homes, and became internal refugees (known as "present absentees"), and their land reverted to the state.

Every country has laws that allow the expropriation of land for reasons of security or for public use. In Israel's case, the state's immoral and racist application of these otherwise necessary and neutral laws constitutes an additional way in which laws and morality come into conflict. Examples include the extensive use of such legislation to designate Palestinian landholdings as military firing zones, nature reserves, or archeological sites, only to allow the establishment of Israeli settlements on the now "empty" land.

In this context, one should mention that the plans for the southern extension to Israel's Road No. 6 were drawn up without taking into consideration its effect on Bedouin communities in the Negev, and will mean the destruction of hundreds of homes. Road-building is yet another way to push more and more Bedouins out of their "unrecognized" villages and into planned townships, where the state would like all Negev Bedouins to be concentrated.

Another example of nationalist-racist use of laws that seem necessary and morally neutral has been the declaring of most of the *sayag* (restricted) area, to which the state transferred the Bedouin who remained in the Negev in the 1950s, as agricultural land where construction is forbidden, thereby rendering all construction in the Bedouin villages there illegal. Israel refused to grant official recognition to those villages that had already existed in the *sayag* area before the establishment of the state, and even the villages that the state itself created when it transferred Bedouins into the area were refused recognition. Thus, political decisions and planning and construction legislation have criminalized an entire population who are simply attempting to realize the fundamental human right to a roof over their heads; all this as a way of pressuring the Bedouins to leave their land and villages and move into the townships - only because they are Bedouins in the "Jewish state." It is commonly said that laws should not be made that the citizens cannot uphold. In the case of the Palestinian citizens of Israel, this principle has long since been abandoned.

Israel has always exploited the fact that many Palestinians refused to register the ownership of their land with the Ottoman "tabu" (Land Registry Office) or, later, with the British Mandate authorities. Their refusal derived from their unwillingness to pay taxes and during Ottoman rule, there was the additional factor that land-registry documents were used to identify potential soldiers to the Ottoman army. So instead, they relied on their traditional approaches to land-ownership. Over time Israel developed the practice of not recognizing this traditional land-ownership and, in this way, appropriated extensive tracts of land. Land that was not privately owned, and had been used primarily as communal pasture land became "state land" – code for its transfer from Palestinian to Jewish ownership and use.

Israel did not learn the right lessons from the discrimination and persecution suffered by generations of Jews. The state's discrimination against and persecution of the country's Palestinian minority shows that what Israel learned from the persecution of the Jews was a "different" lesson; i.e., that it needed to make sure to formulate many of its discriminatory laws in general terms, so they would not appear to be aimed specifically at the population they harm.

Below is a list of several ways in which Israeli laws have come into conflict with morality in the course of the state's dispossession of the country's Palestinian inhabitants and the takeover of their land:

1. A head-on collision between the law and morality, as when a law is passed that directly harms people whose only "sin" is that they are Palestinians in the Jewish state or under its jurisdiction;

2. The nationalistic and racist application of otherwise "neutral" laws in ways that harm people, again, whose only "sin" is being Palestinians under the jurisdiction of the Jewish state;

3. Disregarding traditional land ownership as a way of transferring land from its Palestinian owners to the state;

4. Declaring tracts of land to be "state land," – as previously mentioned, code for the transfer of land from Palestinian to Jewish ownership and use;

5. Denying the ratification of master-plans for Palestinian localities, and consequently refusing to issue building permits to residents of those localities and - when those impacted by this policy are compelled to build without permits - demolishing their homes.

What we are witnessing here is that one side – the stronger side – in the conflict enacts laws that facilitate its endeavors to take the country over from the Palestinian side. Such use of a law, whether direct or indirect, sets it on a collision course with morality and violates the human rights of the Palestinians whose land and homes are taken from them. In addition, these laws result in the perpetration of war crimes by the IDF when it comes to enforce them in the occupied territories and, likewise, by the Israeli Police when they enforce them inside Israel proper. These are both instances where the authorities – through legislation – cause injury to people whose misfortune it is to have been born Palestinian in the Jewish state or under its military occupation.

One could ask what is so terrible about these laws. In response, I would give the example of the Nuremberg Laws of 1935. They revoked the citizenship of Germany's Jews and left them with no legal way to defend themselves. The same applies here. The Palestinians have no effective legal means of prevailing against the harm done to them.

Israel is a democratic state where anyone may appeal to the courts and demand his/her rights. The problem is that one-and-the-same side in the conflict is both the legislator and the judiciary. Thus, the victims of dispossession for the sake of Zionist expansionism have almost no chance of redress in court, when they come to demand justice and their rights.

When the UN General Assembly appealed to the highest judicial authority in the world – the International Court of Justice at The Hague – requesting its opinion on the legality of the construction of the separation barrier in the occupied West Bank, Israel refused to submit its arguments to the court. The fear was that there was no chance that a neutral court – unlike Israel's courts - would accept Israel's claims in this matter. Instead, Israel sent the skeleton of a bus blown up in a suicide bombing to be used in a demonstration outside the courthouse, but did not dare send Israeli legal experts to argue its case before the court, since they understood how little chance their arguments stood of persuading anyone. Indeed, the International Court of Justice (ICJ) ruled, in its July 2004 advisory opinion, that erecting the separation barrier within occupied territory is illegal, since the Fourth Geneva Convention applies throughout the occupied West Bank (including East Jerusalem). This means that all of the Israeli settlements in the occupied territories are illegal, as is any harm done to Palestinian civilians because of the settlements, at the hands of the IDF or settlers.

Back in Israel, the then-presiding chief justice of the Supreme Court, Aharon Barak, executed a brilliant maneuver when he ruled on a petition brought by the Association for Civil Rights in Israel against the route of the separation barrier in the vicinity of the settlement of Alfei Menashe. His decision, delivered only a few days before the ruling by the ICJ, stated that there was no proportionality between Israel's security needs and the harm inflicted upon Palestinian citizens along said route, and that therefore the barrier must be rerouted westward (though not outside the occupied territory). Justice Barak thus created an Israeli precedent prior to the Hague ruling. He also created for himself, as well as for the Israeli court, a "leftist" image as well as a precedent that Israel has used as a pretext for its continued disregard for the advisory opinion of the ICJ and for the continuation of its construction of the separation barrier inside occupied territory.

By the way, it is important to understand that the ICJ, in

its advisory opinion, put an end to the debate between Israel and the rest of the world as to whether or not the Fourth Geneva Convention applies in the occupied territories and East Jerusalem. Israel has persisted in ignoring the ICJ advisory opinion despite the fact that the UN General Assembly acknowledged and affirmed it, as did the Security Council in 2016.

Another occasion when we saw Israel refuse to testify was during the inquiry by the Goldstone Commission (United Nations Fact Finding Mission on the Gaza Conflict) into Israel's assault on Gaza in late 2008 - early 2009, "Operation Cast Lead." There were serious allegations that the Israeli army had committed a long list of war crimes during that operation, and the chairman of the UN Human Rights Council (UNHRC) asked the South African Jewish-Zionist jurist Richard Goldstone to head a commission of inquiry. Judge Goldstone wished to know about the commission's mandate, and after reading it, refused the appointment. The UNHRC chairman then asked Goldstone to write his own proposition for the commission's mandate. The chairman accepted Goldstone's rewritten proposal and appointed him to head the commission. Goldstone's principal change consisted of extending the commission's mandate to encompass the examination of the actions of both sides rather than just Israel's. Indeed, the Goldstone Commission found that not only Israel had committed war crimes, but also Hamas, by its missile attacks targeting Israeli civilians.

As mentioned above, Israel refused to cooperate with the Goldstone Commission. It also refused to allow anyone representing the state to appear before the commission. As far as we Israelis are concerned, we are the only ones permitted to investigate allegations of war crimes committed by Israeli soldiers. As in the case of the separation barrier, here too, Israel complained that the commission's conclusions had not taken its arguments into consideration – arguments which, as stated above, Israel had refused to present.

Israel's refusal to abide by the conclusions reached by the International Court of Justice and the Goldstone Commission, with the complaint that Israel's arguments – which it had refused to present to the commission – had not been given consideration reminds me of the trial of Marwan Barghouti. He was brought to trial in an Israeli military court, on charges of responsibility for the murder of Israelis who had been killed in terrorist attacks. He argued that his trial should take place in a neutral court rather than an Israeli one, since he had a dispute with Israel. After all, if one side brings its own judges to rule between the two sides in the dispute, there is no chance that such a one-sided court would produce a fair judgment. Of course, the court did not give any credence to Marwan Barghouti's stance, and sentenced him to several terms of life imprisonment.

A country can pass whatever laws it pleases. The problem is that when the laws are at odds with morality, they undermine that country's moral standing and their own moral authority. So it was with South Africa's apartheid legislation, the racist "Jim Crow" segregation laws in the US South, and the Nuremberg Laws in Nazi Germany; and so it is in Israel. The more the world becomes aware of the immoral laws – both direct and indirect, both inside Israel and in the occupied territories - the more the country's moral standing is undermined.

THE CASE OF THE NEGEV BEDOUINS

Like the other Palestinians living in the area where the State of Israel was established, most of the Bedouins became refugees as a result of wartime expulsion or flight (1948). The difference is that the State of Israel continued expelling Bedouins for another decade after the signing of the armistice in 1949. Furthermore, to this day Israel continues to turn Bedouins who remained within its borders into internally displaced persons (some of them repeatedly) in an attempt to compel them all to move to the townships that it set up for them. In other words, as far as its Bedouin citizens are concerned, the State of Israel has never implemented the armistice ending the 1948 War, but continues its one-sided war against them.

Here I will present some data and will attempt to describe some of the processes that have taken place over the years:

There is disagreement regarding the number of Bedouins living in the Negev on the eve of the 1948 War. Minimalists speak of 65,000, maximalists of 110,000. What we do know is that the census held in 1960 showed 11,000 Bedouins remaining in the Negev at that time. By 2014 (at time of writing) their number had surpassed 240,000.

The amount of land cultivated by the Bedouins in the Negev prior to the 1948 War is also in dispute, with minimalists speaking of 1,500,000 dunam (approx. 375,000 acres) and maximalists of 3,500,000 dunam (approx. 875,000 acres). In 2014, after being dispossessed of almost all of their land, Bedouins retained control of some 350,000 -400,000 dunam, and another 600,000 dunam were the subject of ongoing land claims suits.

Nearly all of the vast expanses of the Negev used to serve the Bedouins as pasture land, hardly any of which remains in their possession today. For that reason, most Bedouins have ceased to earn their livelihood from sheep and goat herding, although many of them still persevere in keeping a small number of animals for family use, for which they usually must purchase feed. This greatly increases their expenses, rendering the animals' upkeep uneconomical. A major part of the disaster that has been visited upon the Bedouin community (as on the rest of the Palestinian population) is the loss of traditional means of livelihood as a result of the loss of the bulk of their land.

Like all of the Palestinians who remained within Israel's borders after the 1948 War, the Negev Bedouins were subjected to a regime of military government, which was lifted only in late 1966.

In the 1950s, alongside the ongoing expulsion of Bedouins from the country, a policy was instituted of concentrating the remaining Bedouins in the *sayag* zone, located in the north-east of the Negev. Usually the military governor or his representative would come to the *sheikh* of a Bedouin tribe and tell him that the army was preparing to carry out maneuvers in their area. Therefore, "for their own safety," they should move somewhere else. He would promise (orally, not in writing) that in six months, when the maneuvers are over, they would be able to return. They were, however, not permitted to return; instead, the Land Acquisition Law (1953) was passed, enabling the state to transfer much of the "abandoned" land to itself! A clear-cut legislative land-grab! And of course, most of the pasture land, which had not been privately owned, became "state land," code for the transfer of land from traditional use by Bedouins to Jewish ownership. Not only does Israel, which regards land belonging to Bedouin as *mawat* ("dead" or uncultivated) land, treat it as "state land," this position has been reinforced by (Israeli) court rulings that rejected Bedouins' cultivation, traditional deeds, or payment of past taxes as proof of their ownership of this land.

Most of the villages in the *sayag* zone have been there since before the establishment of the state, but Israel itself has chosen not to recognize them. Worse yet, tribes that the state removed from their own land and transferred to the *sayag* zone in the fifties, were not given a legal basis for the new villages they established in the area to which they had been forcibly moved. They were (and still are) treated like interlopers, their villages refused government recognition. Even this was not enough for the state. In 1965 the Knesset (Israeli parliament) passed a Planning and Construction Law to regulate construction and land use throughout the country, as is essential for any modern state. Israel, though, has used this law to designate most of the *sayag* zone as agricultural land, thereby rendering all structures there illegal. I call this a racist use of a neutral law.

When a village is not recognized, it does not appear on the official maps of the country and, consequently, Jewish settlements are sometimes planned for construction in locations where there are existing Bedouin villages. Forests are planned and planted on village land. Highways end up running right through some Bedouin villages. A power plant was even built in the Bedouin village of Wadi Al Na'am. Of course the villagers do not benefit from this, nor do they receive any of the electricity produced there. What they do receive is electromagnetic radiation from the overhead high-tension wires, along with attendant health problems.

In addition, unrecognized villages have no municipal governing bodies and so are not eligible for municipal services, leaving them without running water, electricity, paved streets, garbage collection, or sewers. Children in unrecognized villages now have access to schools, but only after the government was compelled to set them up following an appeal to Israel's High Court of Justice citing the Compulsory Education Law; and these are mostly regional institutions (i.e., one for several villages, requiring sometimes hazardous travel) with only temporary status. Some of the villages have been connected to the national water system. The water reaches storage tanks beside each home through pipes laid by the villagers themselves, filling them one by one. The inhabitants of other villages have to purchase their water and transport it to the village in tanks pulled by tractors. And of course it is impossible to build legally in an unrecognized village, so a Bedouin who wishes to realize his basic human right to a roof over his head and his family is forced to break the law; an estimated 50,000 structures – homes, sheep and goat pens, and storerooms – have been constructed illegally in these villages.

In the 1960s the Israeli government began to implement a new policy: to concentrate the Negev Bedouin population by moving them into townships (making them, once again, internally displaced persons). This is essentially the reason that the government has not recognized their villages. Everything is aimed at pressuring the Bedouins to leave their remaining land, their homes, and their villages, and move into the "concentration towns" built for them by the state. When the Bedouins began being relocated to these townships, there were about 40,000 Bedouins in the Negev. Seven townships were established, in which the state has succeeded in concentrating over half of the Negev Bedouin population (about 60%). These communities suffer from record rates of unemployment, poverty, and crime: a failure by any standard! Nevertheless the Israeli government regards the concentration of all of the rest of the Bedouins in townships as the only option allowing their continued presence in the Negev – simply so that it can grab the rest of their land.

The government tells us that it cannot provide services for every village or collection of buildings, while at the same time allowing the establishment of ranches in the Negev by private individuals, some of them right on land stolen from Bedouins, and each of which covers hundreds or thousands of dunams. These have been built illegally, and naturally all of them belong to Jews. Sorry – my mistake. One ranch is owned by a Bedouin and covers all of four dunams (i.e., one acre)! Not to worry! The Knesset has passed all the necessary laws to render the illegally set up ranches "kosher," and every one of these ranches has running water, electricity, and an access road. By contrast, a Bedouin village with a population in the thousands cannot obtain any such amenities.

They tell us that modernization necessitates the relocation of the Bedouins to the townships. My experience tells me otherwise. I recall having initiated a protest at an unrecognized Bedouin village where we were going to plant wheat in the traditional manner. When we got to the field, I asked our Bedouin hosts to teach us the proper, traditional way of doing it. Not one of them knew how. On the other hand, right beside us stood a modern tractor equipped with a large seed-planting machine capable of sowing more seed in five minutes than we could by hand in an hour. In fact, most of my Bedouin friends are far more adept than I at using the computer, smartphone, and other such modern technological devices. Since the state denies them electricity, Bedouins in the unrecognized villages have to use generators for power. The high cost of this electricity restricts its use to only a few early evening hours. Over the years, I have seen more and more Bedouins using solar collectors and storage batteries to provide them with round-the-clock electricity. They don't need to move into the townships for the sake of "modernization."

Israel demolishes hundreds of Bedouin homes a year, razes entire villages, destroys thousands of dunams of Bedouin crops, and limits their access to pasture land; all of this in an attempt to pressure them to give up their remaining land, leave their villages, and move into the concentration townships. When even these measures didn't have the desired effect, the government resolved to speed up the process of concentrating the Bedouins in townships, first of all by intensifying enforcement. This increased the number of house demolitions in the Negev by hundreds a year.

In 2008, a commission was set up to study the issues and to make policy recommendations. The nine-member Goldberg Commission included two Bedouin members. Although a small minority, they wrote a strongly worded statement of their reservations regarding the commission's conclusions. Under the pretext that an implementation plan was required for the Goldberg Commission's recommendations, the Prawer Plan - for the transfer of the remainder of the Bedouin population to the existing townships and to a number of others yet to be built – was drafted. A legislative process was initiated with the aim of completing the concentration of the Bedouins and settling their land ownership issues within three years.

By the way, this legislation targeting Bedouins strongly resembles South Africa's apartheid laws. In the past, whenever Israel had made laws for the purpose of robbing Palestinian citizens of their land or to violate their civil rights, it had always maintained the appearance that these were laws applicable to the general population. In this case, the state broke with longstanding custom in a blatant attempt to pass legislation specifically injurious to the Negev Bedouins. The intended outcome of the Prawer Plan and the associated legislation is that some 40,000 Bedouins are to be ejected from their homes, villages, and land and relocated to the townships, and dozens of villages are to be wiped off the map. In order to carry out this plan, the state created a special police unit, called "Yoav," among whose duties are the provision of "security" during the demolition of homes and villages and the destruction of crops that accompany the concentration of all the remaining Bedouins in the townships allotted them by the Jewish State. So now there is a special police unit whose role is to persecute those Israeli citizens whose only crime is to have been born Bedouin in the Jewish State.

Here it is important to take a closer look at the issue of land ownership. I'll begin by saying that prior to 1948, the Negev was divided into a number of Bedouin tribal territories (see accompanying map). Each was home to several extended families, all of which inhabited their own respective lands, which they owned according to traditional practice. In the dry seasons, they would take their herds to graze a long distance from their home territory, and would return there for the winter.

In 1858 the Ottoman rulers passed the Land Code, requiring every landowner to register his property in the *tabu*, the official property registry, so that the government could tax them accordingly. The overwhelming majority of Bedouins (as well as many Palestinian peasant farmers) refused to register their ownership of land in the Ottoman registry. For the Bedouins, traditional ownership laws were sufficient. In any case, paying taxes on arid desert land was difficult. Moreover, the land registry rolls were used to draft landowners into the Ottoman Army.

In fact, in the early 20th century, when the Ottoman rulers decided to turn Beer Sheva (Beersheba) into the seat of regional government, it purchased land from the Bedouins in accordance with their traditional land-ownership laws. Even the Zionist Movement, prior to 1948, bought land from Bedouins in the Negev under these traditional laws, and founded several kibbutzim there. The British Mandate authorities, too, respected the Bedouins' traditional ownership.

On the other hand, the State of Israel decided not to recognize the Bedouins' traditional ownership of their land, and created a legal precedent to that effect. Israel only recognizes ownership registered in the Ottoman *tabu* or of land that has been under continuous cultivation; and to this end Bedouins are obliged to prove that there was a community on that spot in 1858. There is, therefore, virtually no chance that a Bedouin can prove his ownership of land in an Israeli court. Even when he has documents that record the purchase of the land and the payment of taxes on it, he is helpless before the legal precedents that have been set.

It is important to note that in the early 1970s, Israel gave Bedouins the opportunity to register their ownership claims. Thirty-two hundred did so, their claims totalling one-and-a-half million dunams. The state refused to accept claims for pasture land, and thus reduced the amount of land eligible for claim by half-a-million dunams. Then, pursuant to a political decision, Israel avoided dealing with the settlement of these ownership claims for some thirty years. During that time, many of the claimants who were well acquainted with boundaries of their properties died, leaving heirs who were much less knowledgeable… Only then did the state begin to declare its ownership of these very same pieces of land, challenging the Beduoins' claims in court. Up to now, the state has always won its petitions and has transferred into its ownership much of the abovementioned land (of approximately 400 claims, 200 have so far ended with the state winning title to 70,000 dunams).

In the State of Israel's war against its own Bedouin citizens, again, we see instances of the clash between law and morality of which I have written earlier. Israel is a democratic state, where any Bedouin is entitled to take his concerns to court. The problem is that one side in the conflict is both legislator and architect of the legal structure designed to serve it; and this same side also appoints the judges who rule on its disputes with the Bedouins. So of course, Bedouins have next to no chance of success in Israeli courts of law.

To those who do not know all of the above, the government's argument – that the Bedouins are criminals violating the law

– might well appear to be correct. If we recall how we got to this point, though, we will understand that the real criminals here are all of Israel's governments, past and present, and not their victims – the Bedouins. That is, Israel's governments and Knesset have created a clear contradiction between law and morality. After stealing nearly all of the Bedouins' land and not recognizing their traditional ownership over the little that remains, the state claims that the Bedouins have been taking over state land!

It is commonly accepted that in every society there is a certain percentage of criminals. But when everyone is a "criminal," the problem is with the law! Israel made the politically motivated decision to avoid recognizing Bedouin villages that had been in the same place since prior to the establishment of the state. On top of that, it refrained from creating any legal basis for the villages which it itself created when it transferred tribes from their traditional land to the *sayag* zone, where it now claims they are interlopers. Moreover, in order to "concentrate" the Bedouins, it has employed planning and construction laws to designate the *sayag* zone land as agricultural, where construction is prohibited; so that any Bedouin in the villages who wishes to realize his basic human right to shelter is compelled to violate Israeli law! After all of this, the state creates a special police unit whose job is to wage war on the Bedouins who break its thieving, racist laws. The clash between law and morality in this case finds expression in the actions of these police when they enforce immoral laws. The police – by demolishing homes and villages and destroying crops, instead of fighting crime - are themselves committing crimes in the name of the law.

The question begging to be asked is why the Bedouins have "deserved" harsher treatment than the rest of the Palestinians who remained in Israel proper following the 1948 War and became Israeli citizens. It seems to me that there are three main reasons. Firstly, they have always lived on the periphery, far from the "public eye," so that this policy did not come up against local or international opposition. The second reason is that in the minds of Jewish Israelis, Bedouins are perceived as nomads; so what does it matter if they are moved around? Thirdly, even in Palestinian society, Bedouins are low on the social scale. For many years, there was hardly any involvement by other Palestinian citizens of Israel in Bedouin affairs. Only with the intensification of the home demolition policy and the forced removal of Bedouins to the townships has there been an increase in the involvement of Palestinians from the northern part of the country in protecting Bedouin rights in the Negev.

Finally I want propose a simple mental exercise: Let us imagine that any country in the world treated its Jewish minority the way Israel has been treating its Bedouin minority. In order to "protect" the Jews, they would be concentrated in their own townships. In order to encourage them to move, their homes would be demolished, their businesses boycotted, municipal services denied them, and so forth. I am certain we would all be enraged and protest vociferously, accusing that country of anti-Semitism. The government of Israel would immediately recall its ambassador and demand that the UN order that country to halt the implementation of this policy. It is therefore fitting that we go back and examine where we ourselves stand when our own state implements anti-Semitic policies against the Bedouin minority in our midst.

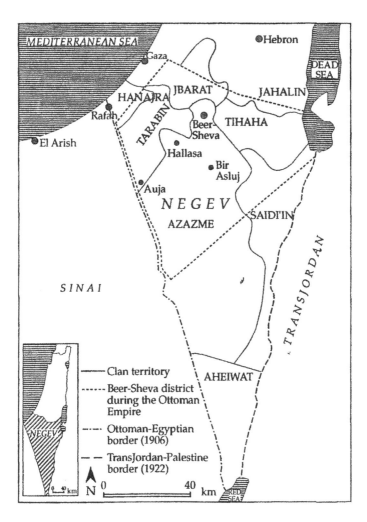

FIGURE 4.1 Clan, administrative, and international borders in the Negev in the early twentieth century (*Source:* Adapted from Bar-Zvi and Ben-David 1978).

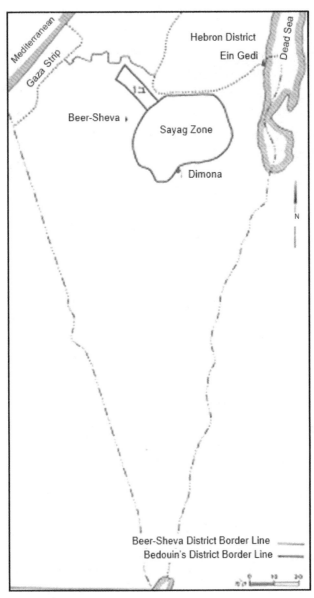

The Sayag Zone (Yosef Ben David (1996), Controversy in
the Negev: Bedouins, Jews and Lands [Hebrew])

HOW CRIMINALIZATION OF THE VICTIM IS DONE

It is interesting to see how the process of criminalizing the victim works. We shall examine this via the situation of the Bedouin in the Negev and the case of Sheikh Sayyakh of El Araqib, and also how it is done to the Palestinians in the occupied territories.

For hundreds, perhaps thousands of years, Bedouin have lived in the Negev. Due to the wilderness conditions, a nomadic, and later a semi-nomadic, way of life developed. There are permanent settlements where they stay on their lands during the rainy season, while during the dry season part or all of the family is on the move in search of pasture lands for the sheep and goats. To the best of my knowledge none of the historic rulers of the land interfered with the Bedouins' unique way of life - until the establishment of the State of Israel.

In the 1948 War of Independence most of the Bedouin were expelled from the country. The expulsions continued after the 1949 ceasefire until 1959. In the 1950s most of the Bedouin who remained in the country were concentrated in the Sayyag region in the Negev, located south of the West Bank. Israel refused to recognize the Bedouin communities that existed prior to the establishment of the state, and refused to grant legal status to the villages it created when it moved the tribes to the Sayyag area – a move which entailed the loss of their lands. Most of the areas in the Negev that had been used for pasture were confiscated and declared off limits to the Bedouin. The end of the 1960s saw the beginning of the policy of concentrating all the Negev Bedouin into townships. In other words, Israel is the first local power to critically damage the existence and unique way of life of the Negev Bedouin.

Like every society, we Israelis tell ourselves that we are the good guys and our enemies are the bad guys. So what can we do when, according to every criterion, what we have been doing to the Bedouin is criminal... and we are the bad guys and they are the victims? We create a legal façade and story which turns the original population of the Negev into criminals when they try to preserve their lands and way of life. I call this the criminalization of the victim.

After the establishment of the state a military government was imposed on all Arab citizens who remained in Israel. This limited the Bedouins' ability for seasonal wandering with their herds. In addition, wide areas in the Negev were closed for pasturing when Israel confiscated these areas and transferred them to state ownership by means of various laws.

Unlike previous rulers of the country, the Israeli government refuses to recognize traditional Bedouin land ownership. Only the official Ottoman-period land registration is recognized. Relying on traditional ownership, the great majority of Bedouins did not officially register their lands. Thus the story was created in Israeli courts that the Bedouin are nomads, not semi-nomads, and as such have no connection to the land. Only if they can prove that they have continuously lived on the land since 1858 – when the Ottomans passed their land law – is their right to the land recognized. Since the Bedouin have no written history, no one can prove such continuous settlement in an Israeli court. And so it is that every Bedouin who insists on holding on to his land becomes a criminal. How does this tally with the fact that the Zionist movement bought lands from Bedouin in the Negev before the establishment of the state on the basis of traditional ownership?

In addition to the non-recognition of their villages, most of the land in the Sayyag area, with the aid of building and planning laws, has been declared agricultural land where construction is prohibited. Thus a situation has been created whereby every Bedouin who fulfills his human right to a roof over his head in his village becomes a criminal! And, until today, the state continues to create internal refugees as Bedouin are driven out of their villages and into the Negev townships. Only there do they cease to be criminals.

All this is accompanied by government and media propaganda which states that the Bedouin are infiltrating state lands and building their homes illegally. If you are ignorant of the historical facts, then these government claims are correct. And in fact most Israeli Jews believe this.

The Hebrew media too plays a part in the criminalization of the Bedouin Negev. It ignores the constant demolition of Bedouin homes and doesn't report them. It ignores the destruction of Bedouin crops every winter and doesn't report them. And in the rare cases where they are reported, the government narrative is adopted and the Bedouin are presented as criminals. All this is done while ignoring the truism that there is a certain percentage of criminals in every population. When the entire population is criminal, this is a sign that the problem is with the laws and not with those who break them. And since criminals must be fought, the police Yoav Unit was created to enforce the law on this "criminal" population - whose only crime is that they are Bedouins in the Jewish state.

Despite the fact that the question of the ownership of his land in the village of El Araqib in the Negev is still awaiting a court decision, the Beersheba District Court ruled that Bedouin Sheikh Sayyakh is a criminal deserving of a 10-month prison sentence. His crime: he refuses to accept the theft of his land and the destruction of his village. He insists on living on his land and preserving his traditional way of life. This makes him a criminal in the State of Israel.

The government of Israel follows a similar policy in the occupied West Bank. There the Israeli army (IDF) systematically acts to take control of the territories while pushing the Palestinians into ever shrinking enclaves. This stands in direct opposition to morality, military and war ethics and to international law.

In this situation as well, it is clear that Israel is the villain, but here too Israelis tell themselves that they are the good guys and their enemies the bad guys. Here too, in order to present their version of events and solve their ethical problem, a legal and security façade has been created in which the IDF carries out a unilateral war against a defenseless population, whose only crime is that they are Palestinians under Israeli rule. In order to overcome the moral and ethical problems, many oppressive acts are presented as law enforcement. This is done by means of orders issued by the military commander of the occupied territories. For this purpose lawyers are employed to formulate the orders in the form of laws. Naturally, the Palestinian victims of these "laws" have no possibility of influencing them. We and the soldiers are told that they are enforcing the law; the reality is that soldiers are being sent to fight a unilateral war against an occupied civilian population.

By means of very creative interpretations of the law the IDF has declared wide areas of the West Bank as "state lands" – a code name for their transfer from Palestinian use to Israeli use. Lands are also declared as firing zones, nature preserves and archaeological sites – all of which serve as means of widespread control over land. And only recently a new legal interpretation has given legal legitimacy to the takeover of privately-owned Palestinian lands.

The IDF dispersed the local building and planning committees and took over all planning authority for Palestinian communities in Area C of the West Bank. In the vast majority of cases the IDF refuses to prepare or confirm building plans for Palestinian communities and grants practically no building permits to Palestinians. When they then have no choice but to build without a permit, the army comes and demolishes their houses in the name of "the law."

The IDF has created a situation in regions such as the South Hebron Hills, areas east of Jerusalem, and the Jordan Valley such that the very existence of these small communities - which were there before the occupation – turns their inhabitants into criminals who are destined to be evacuated. In addition, they have been prevented from grazing their herds in their traditional pasture areas. All of the Palestinian communities in Area C of the West Bank are unable to develop naturally because the IDF does not allow any legal construction there.

In the areas where IDF activity is restricted, settlers are sent to do the job. They attack Palestinian farmers on their agricultural lands and pasture lands, and occasionally also inside their villages. The IDF, instead of expelling the settler attackers and arresting them, protects them and allows them to drive the Palestinians off their land. The police are almost always successful in **not** catching the criminals. If they are pushed, by international pressure, to make arrests - it turns out that most of the time there is not enough evidence to convict. And if they have no choice but to convict - it turns out that the judges and prison authorities are mercifully lenient.

In order to complete this false legal façade, Israel opened its courtrooms to the occupied Palestinian population. There, by means of very creative legal interpretations, assent is given to actions that stand in direct contradiction to international law. It is enough simply to mention the prohibition on transferring the population of the occupying power to the territory occupied: on this basis all of the settlements in the occupied territories are illegal. This also applies to the prohibition of activities harmful to the occupied population (except in cases where clear cut security needs allow it). And thus, an advisory opinion issued by the International Court of Justice in The Hague in 2004 ruled, among other things, that the Fourth Geneva Conventions applied to the West Bank and that, therefore, even the security measures taken by Israel to protect its settlement project are not legal. Israel just ignores all this, as long as it receives the backing of the United States.

As in the case of the Negev Bedouin, in the West Bank too the Hebrew media, for the most part, cooperates with the authorities and avoids reporting on the daily repression of the occupied population. And here too, in the rare instances where it does report, it generally reports the army's and the settlers' version of events. The few journalists who do report the constant attacks on the Palestinians are called traitors, as are human rights and peace activists. They, after all, tell the Israelis what's really happening – a reality most Israelis don't want to know.

On the other hand, in cases where Negev Bedouin or Palestinians from the occupied territories hurt Jewish Israelis, the media blows up the story. In our Jewish consciousness, we are the victims. It doesn't matter how much we subjugate and oppress the Palestinians – most of us refuse to see this – we are the victims of their incomprehensible murderous violence!

THE NATURE OF THE CONFLICT

The Israeli-Palestinian-Arab conflict has its origins in the invasion by members of one society of another society's territory and the systematic expulsion of the latter. Those whom they have not succeeded in pushing out of the country are being squeezed into a continually shrinking space. This is what the fight is about.

Nor is it the first conflict of its kind. We need only recall the European white man's invasion of America and their displacement of its indigenous inhabitants, whether through genocide or by crowding them into ever smaller spaces. So too in Australia and New Zealand, where the white man overran the country, forcing the indigenous peoples on to ever-smaller pieces of land, and in southern Africa, where we saw the same process at work.

In the cases of America and Australia, the newcomers took control of entire continents, and they overran New Zealand in its entirety. In Israel, as in South Africa and Rhodesia, they initially took over a relatively small portion of the land. In all of these cases, the European invaders had the technological upper hand, which translated into military might, and they were better organized and more united than the locals, whom they were therefore able to defeat, despite being outnumbered. It usually took an indigenous population quite a while to comprehend that they were facing an invasion that would not end with the current arrivals, but would continue and would eventually jeopardize their continued presence on their home territory. Due to this delay in recognizing the actual situation, local resistance to the invasions generally was delayed as well.

In all such cases, the invaders' ability to maintain their hegemony over time is dependent on the size of the pool of willing immigrants to the invaded territory, as well as the support and backing available to them from their lands of origin or other countries. Similarly, it can be said that a local population's chance of surviving, or even of halting, the waves of immigration to their territory depends on the support and backing that they have. Once the whites had successfully taken control of the entire North American continent, its indigenous peoples had no one left to help them stem the flow of European immigrants, and white rule was assured. So it was in Australia and New Zealand, too, where whites took over the entire countries, thereby securing their rule.

In the case of South Africa and Rhodesia, where whites gained control of limited areas and lacked the human reserves that might allow them to take over all of Africa, their rule was limited, as well. By contrast, the local inhabitants still had vast support on the rest of the African continent. Following the Second World War, we saw the fall of colonialism. It was in this context that Rhodesia fell, and Zimbabwe arose on the territory that had been Southern Rhodesia (as in 1964, Northern Rhodesia had become Zambia). The whites who remained in Zimbabwe were integrated into the new state.

Among the lessons of the Second World War was a growing awareness of the necessity of fighting racism and of the importance of universal human rights. By the 1990s, this had contributed to a significant reduction in the level of backing and support enjoyed by the whites in southern Africa. Their western supporters could no longer reconcile themselves to the racist laws and accompanying human rights abuses of apartheid-era South Africa. This was why the boycott of South Africa was so effective. I assume that South Africa could have withstood the boycott from an economic point of view. It could not, however, endure the disappearance of its international backing and support. This, in my opinion, was the decisive factor that brought about the abolition of apartheid. This took place despite the fact that whites in South Africa had all the advantages that make for a successful occupation: technological superiority translated into military supremacy (even a nuclear arsenal), better organization, and unity. Altogether, apartheid South Africa's advantages were very similar to Israel's over the Palestinians and Arabs in general.

It is also interesting to compare the two models for the dismantling of white rule in southern Africa – in Rhodesia, and in South Africa - although they were similar in that they integrated the whites into the new states rather than partitioning the countries, At a certain point, blacks in Zimbabwe began repossessing land that whites had earlier taken control of. This resulted in a mass exodus of whites, and played an important role in Zimbabwe's subsequent economic collapse. It seems to me that more of an attempt was made in South Africa to integrate the whites and to proceed towards a shared future, in the hope that this would help the economy to prosper.

The whites in South Africa had different objectives than did the Zionists in Israel. The former took over land where black Africans were living and forced them to leave, but did not expel them from the country. Instead, they used them as a cheap labor force. This resulted in a situation where the white minority ruled a state with a black majority. In Israel, most of the Palestinian-Arab majority was expelled, in hopes of leaving the land solely for the Jews. And in Israel proper, a clear Jewish majority was, indeed, achieved. In the occupied Palestinian territories, the majority is still Palestinian, and Israel's backers and supporters will not tolerate another mass expulsion of Palestinians - in this case, from the West Bank and Gaza Strip. This explains Israel's efforts to retain control of Area C- where the Jewish population is approaching majority status – while designating areas A and B as Palestinian "Bantustans." The Palestinians whom they did not succeed in pushing out of the country constituted a cheap labor force for Israel and Israeli settlements/colonies in Area C. However, due to the problem with security caused by the ongoing battle over land in the occupied territories, Israel eventually resorted to bringing in migrants from Europe and Asia to replace Palestinian laborers. It is interesting to note that this all took place during the years of the Oslo "Peace" Process. It had a seriously damaging effect on the Palestinian economy, whereas this same process promoted the burgeoning of the Israeli economy. These differences between Israel and southern Africa do not, however, detract from the importance of outside backing and support for survival in either instance.

One thing that Israel learned from the South African experience was to formulate its laws so as not to reveal their racist-nationalistic character. The expulsion of Palestinians has been implemented gradually and with minimal fatalities, save for periods of open warfare, when Israel sows death and destruction on a massive scale. Thus, Israel long succeeded in misleading its backers and supporters with regards to what it's been up to. Eventually, as its expansionist policies continued – and right-wing governments have been far more open about this – its racist and nationalistic nature and its systematic injury to Palestinians has come to light, increasingly alienating Israel's traditional supporters. Although there remains, amongst supporters of Israel, consensus in support of the state's survival, there is near consensus in opposition to the occupation and its accompanying violations of human rights, and growing support for the Palestinians' right to a state of their own.

The PLO's recognition of this worldwide state of affairs was the principal reason for its turning to a political path, making a historic compromise with Israel. On the other hand, Hamas and other Palestinian Islamic fundamentalist movements are undermining the Palestinians' ability to weaken backing and support for Israel – by enabling Israel to draw parallels between its struggle against Islamic terrorism and the struggle by a West fearful of an Islamic fundamentalist onslaught on the Christian world and western civilization and of ongoing anti-West Islamic terrorism.

Just as, in the cold war era, Israel developed a special relationship with the US and western Europe based on serving their interests in opposition to the USSR, Israel now tries to serve American and European interests in the Muslim-Christian "clash of civilizations". When the US attempts to separate its war on terror from its relations with Islamic countries, this leads to a confrontation between Israel and the US which affects the special relationship between these two countries, and weakens US backing for Israel.

The ongoing occupation and Israel's growing involvement in the occupied territories is bringing Israel closer to a South

African situation: in place of two states, heading towards a single state with Palestinian Bantustans alongside it. Just as South Africa's backers and supporters could no longer go along with this arrangement, Israel's backers and supporters are ending their acquiescence, as well.

If Israel wishes to survive, it must stop expelling Palestinians from the country, put an end to the occupation by means of peace agreements with its neighbors, start acting in accordance with the norms of international law and human rights conventions, and terminate its racist-nationalistic policies regarding the Palestinian citizens of Israel. Only thus can Israel ensure the continued support of its backers, so vital to its survival. The longer Israel persists in its expansionist policies, the more it weakens own its backing and support, not only regarding the occupation, but also for its very existence: because of the all-encompassing nature of the conflict, disappearance of Israel's support and backing is liable to affect not only the occupation, but the very survival of Israel as a nation-state.

THE RISE AND FALL OF THE SOCIALIST MOVEMENT

Any ideological movement dedicated to correcting the ills of society (socialism, pacifism, the peace movement, anarchism, etc.) strives to make itself obsolete. If, for example, we achieve peace, the peace movement will no longer be necessary. Thus, following the end of the cold war and the dissolution of the USSR, we saw many of the European and North American peace movements either disband or become dramatically smaller. I believe that this is largely what happened to the socialist movement in its various iterations, and I wish to offer my interpretation of how this took place.

Socialist ideas date back to ancient times, but not until the industrial revolution did they give rise to mass movements. The explanation for this, in my opinion, is that even during the horrendously cruel times of slavery and feudalism, slaves and serfs had a measure of security; it was in the interest of the slave owner to keep his slaves alive and able to work, since his survival depended on their labor. So, too, the survival of the feudal lord was dependent on the ability of his serfs to do the work required to maintain the estate.

The industrial revolution saw the onset of mass migrations from rural areas into urban centers in the search for work. Those who found jobs were employed under harsh conditions at starvation wages. The state of the unemployed was even worse. In fact, a whole social class was created that no one had an interest in providing for. That was the historical moment when socialist ideas went from being lofty abstractions to responding to a concrete need, as an entire social class began to see socialism as serving its interests. Socialist movements sprang up in many countries and began to struggle for the rights of both the workers and the unemployed, out of an understanding that only solidarity would give them sufficient power and influence both to improve working conditions and to provide for those without work.

Over the years, we have seen the emergence of two principal attitudes shared by a wide variety of socialist movements:

The first is that capitalism is evil by nature and must therefore be brought down in a revolution and be replaced by a society based upon socialist principles. The second argues that change should take place through an evolutionary process within the existing system. The first position was espoused by communists, anarchists and, here in Israel, the kibbutz and Moshav movements, as well. The second was advocated by social-democratic and socialist political parties the world over. These worked to generate change within the system, and created the welfare state as the outcome of a compromise between the socialists and capitalists, who feared that if they didn't compromise, there might well be a revolution, which would bring about their demise.

The communists successfully staged revolutions in several countries, and forcibly imposed their way upon the population. In many cases this involved a reign of terror, which made things even worse than under the capitalism it replaced. The kibbutzim and moshavim and, in certain cases, the anarchists (e.g., in Spain) presented a different model of revolutionary change: voluntary revolution, carried out only by those who embraced it of their own free will, in the hope that their success would encourage more and more people to join them, until their vision prevailed throughout the entire society. This form of revolution would not impose itself upon the unwilling. The moral difference between the two types of revolution is obvious. In the kibbutzim, this lack of compulsion is reflected in the relatively large proportion of those who tried out that way of life but then chose to leave.

The kibbutzim aroused much appreciation and interest as an alternative to the capitalist order, but without the horrors of communist regimes. This was not only because of their important role in nation-building, but also because of the significance for humanity of their way of life. Even so, they did not succeed in turning their project into a nation-wide revolution, and have remained islands in a capitalist sea.

Socialist movements in western countries set up social safety nets for all of their citizens. They produced a national ideal different from that of the capitalist right. Instead of the fear and xenophobia upon which right-wing nationalism was based, the socialists proposed caring for everyone in the country and ensuring their economic survival – as a central component of their nationalism. There are, of course, additional factors in forging a national identity, such as shared myths, but in this I don't see very much difference between right and left.

The achievements of the early socialist movements were followed, in the second and third generations, by a decrease in ideological fervor once survival was assured. As in the case of the peace movements that ceased to exist once peace was achieved, so too the socialists' success in assuring economic sustenance for all was followed by a weakening of support for the movement. And indeed, the era from the nineteen seventies to the present has seen the fall of the majority of communist regimes. Social-democratic parties have begun to participate in the privatization processes and erosion of the welfare state in their respective countries. In Israel we have seen the moshav movement abandon its ideals and collapse, followed by the disintegration of the kibbutz movement. In other words, we were transformed from an ideologically committed society to a hedonistic one, uninvolved in grand ideologies.

We are currently witnessing the decline of the welfare state, with the loss of the universal social safety nets that it provided. As a result, we see a steady rise in poverty, even in times of economic prosperity. Naturally this prompts the question of whether this process will return the socialist movement to its days of glory or if a different variety of socialism will arise to take up the fight for assured sustenance for all. At the moment, the issues of universal food security, a living wage, and universal health care are part and parcel of the struggle for human rights.

The protest movement that rose and fell in Israel in 2011 underscored the great changes experienced by the socialist movement in the course of Israeli society's transition from ideological commitment to hedonism. Inspired by the "Arab Spring," this was a mass movement with the potential for enormous change. However, even its leaders were not clear about their goals, so they turned to university professors for help in formulating their demands of the government.

This movement had been launched by middle class young people who sensed the imminent loss of their economic status. They neither represented the poorer sectors of Israeli society, nor did they commit themselves to the struggle of those sectors or make any effort to include them. As members of a hedonistic society, they lacked the stamina for a long, exhausting struggle. Apparently, in the absence of an ideology with its theoretical underpinnings - laying bare the inherent ills of the capitalist system - and without the stamina required for extended struggles, no social change movement stands a chance of having a serious impact on our lives.

Israeli society's shift from ideological commitment to hedonism also had a negative impact on the peace movement, especially its moderate majority. There used to be a kind of correlation between socialism and aspirations for peace. The majority of the supporters of Israeli peace groups tended to come from the political left. That is also why, to this very day, Israeli "peaceniks" are referred to as "lefties." Apparently those who maintain the value of human life as a principle, and regard the state as providing the mechanism for people's survival, are also more sensitive to issues of quality of life; and it is easier for them to regard everyone's quality of life as taking priority over individual profit. We can see this trend reflected in the political positions taken by left-wing parties in Israel. *Hadash*, basically a Communist-led coalition, is more radical on peace issues as well as social ones. *Meretz*, the party of the Zionist left, is less radical on both social and peace issues than *Hadash* and more radical than the Labor Party in both areas.

In contrast to the move to hedonism by much of Israel's left, there remains a very high level of commitment amongst the Zionist zealots. Besides their active involvement in the settlement movement, the zealots have infiltrated all of the relevant ruling institutions, where they consistently and efficiently promote their own agenda. Exploiting the fact that the existential Zionist mainstream had, like them, adopted a policy of territorial expansion, the zealots forged a single-issue coalition with them. This alliance broke down – and was replaced by open hostility between the two factions - when the central, existential, stream of Zionism, under heavy pressure from the US, embarked upon "the peace process."

The Israeli army is one of the places where the country's shift from commitment to hedonism is most obvious. In the past, the percentage of kibbutz and moshav members in elite combat units far exceeded their percentage in the general population. Today we see, instead, that the younger generation of Zionist zealots are serving in those same units at a rate much higher than their share of the population. This increases the danger that, at some critical juncture, they may well obey their rabbis rather than the country's elected leaders. Should the Israeli government, bowing to external pressure, choose the path of peace, there is a distinct danger that the Zionist zealots would rebel and escalate their opposition to peace even to the point of civil war. I regard the assassination of Prime Minister Rabin in 1995 as the first shot in this war.

When it comes to events of great consequence, I believe it is important to learn from past experience and to discern how we may preserve the values of ideological movements such as socialism. Much diminished as their strength may be, their ideological underpinnings could still provide the infrastructure for future social and political change.

LEARNING FROM MARTIN LUTHER KING JR.'S SUCCESSFUL NON-VIOLENT STRUGGLE

We tend to think that we should learn from our failures. In the case of the peace and human rights movement, generally a minority, I believe one should also learn from successes. In this context, it would be interesting to look at why the US Civil Rights Movement led by Dr. Martin Luther King Jr succeeded in influencing American society as strongly as it did. After all, at about the same time, the Black Panthers, who took the opposite approach to that of Dr. King, were also active in the US. Both movements energetically opposed racism in the US. The first did so nonviolently, whereas the second advocated violent resistance.

If we look at attitudes towards violence in human society, we see that its use is generally regarded as immoral, in and of itself. Hence, anyone who accepts the norms of his/her society, needs to justify his/her "immoral" actions when resorting to violence. We see this even among small children. Let us take an incident where two children are hitting each other. The kindergarten teacher arrives and separates them. Each child accuses the other of "starting it." In other words, his justification for resorting to violence was that the other child was violent towards him or otherwise harmed him, forcing him to defend himself. This dynamic is also at work in international conflicts, among others. Every party that resorts to violence claims that this was in response to the violence or other form of injury inflicted by the other. When we turn to nonviolence, we short circuit our opponents' ability to justify their use of violence by claiming that it was a response to our violence against them. If they persist in employing violence despite this, they lose their moral standing with those who are not involved in the conflict and, eventually, in their own community as well.

The Black Panthers maintained that because racism is violent, it was their right to resist it with violence. They were expressing the widespread belief that violence justifies counter-violence. Indeed the ongoing harm inflicted upon people whose only "crime" is their skin color - and who can do nothing to change the way they are treated by changing their behavior – has always been intolerable. The problem is that whites were and still are the majority in the general US population, as well as in the country's governing bodies, and they have a monopoly on official violent force – through control of the police and military – as a part of their dominance. This has allowed them to relatively easily suppress the blacks' violent struggles, while their own violence was perceived as legitimate and as necessary for preservation of the status quo. The Black Panthers succeeded in garnering the support of the white radical left, but they did not succeed in gaining the sympathy of the moderate mainstream.

By contrast, the Civil Rights Movement's use of nonviolence eliminated any justification for the exercise of violence against the black protesters. It is important to remember that most whites at the time regarded blacks in negative terms, as criminals, violent people, rapists, and as lazy and dangerous. Oppressors always view their victims in this way. I call this, "criminalization of the victim." After all, they must justify their own conduct to themselves. As soon as the blacks, by virtue of their use of nonviolent struggle, had liberated the whites from their fears, the whites could no longer justify their own violence. Thus the blacks succeeded in altering the whites' attitudes towards them. They also successfully made it clear to the world who were the real victims and who the violent, criminal oppressors - revealing to the whites the horrific injustice of their treatment of blacks.

In other words, only when the white oppressors were freed from their fears of the oppressed blacks could they see the terrible injustices that they had inflicted upon the latter. That was when more and more whites began to support the black struggle and even to actively join it. Now they could struggle against unjust, racist laws and for the blacks' human rights without feeling that they were jeopardizing the security of the white community. Through nonviolent struggle, the Civil Rights Movement succeeded in penetrating to the heart of the white mainstream to such an extent that it even received support from the federal government.

So too in the Israeli-Palestinian conflict, we see a similar dynamic in reaction to violent responses by Palestinians to their being forced out of the country. Palestinian violence initially helped bring their plight to the attention of the world. However, as soon as there is violence by Palestinians, it is regarded as legitimizing Israeli violence. Given the existing state of extreme imbalance between the military strengths of the two sides, it is very easy for Israel to quell any resistance while at the same time portraying the matter as a case of self-defence against murderous terrorism that is inimical to its survival. And indeed, the occupier can present the entire struggle as self-defence against terrorism being inflicted upon innocent civilians by a demonic foe. The whole discourse becomes focused on the occupier's "security," whereas the occupied, whose security is almost totally disregarded, are portrayed not as victims, but as a "problem." Now they are the threat to security! In the case of violence by Palestinians, as with violence by US blacks, it is only amongst members of the radical left that this form of struggle has found support. As far as the mainstream and ruling establishments in the West go, it has merely increased support for Israel.

As was the case with blacks in the US, I believe that Palestinian nonviolence would change the picture here. A fully nonviolent struggle on the part of the Palestinians would eliminate any justification for Israeli violence and would clarify which side was the assailant and which the victim; who's security has been ignored and who has done the ignoring. If Israelis no longer feared for their security, it would be easier for them to actually see the horrific injustice they have inflicted upon the Palestinians. It would also begin to be clearer to Israel's backers and supporters who the aggressor is and who the victim, and who is occupying and expelling whom.

Even today, with the decreased level of Palestinian violence, we can see a change taking place amongst Israel's western backers and supporters: The BDS movement has been increasingly gaining support and chalking up numerous victories. More and more countries are openly declaring their support for the Palestinians' right to a state of their own. If the Palestinians adopt total nonviolence, this process will accelerate and will enable them to more easily gain the support of ruling establishments in the West. I believe that even the ruling bodies in Israel itself will find it easier to accommodate them.

We have seen how Israel uses the violence exercised by Hamas and other Palestinian groups as a pretext for presenting itself as a frontline actor in the struggle against Islamic terrorism. The armed struggle that these groups wage against Israel is frightening and damaging, but it does not really threaten the state's existence, and is used to justify Israeli violence against Palestinians. We have seen this in the warfare of Hamas and others in Gaza against Israel. The rockets fired at Israel have taken few lives and destroyed little property. Israel, on the other hand, has killed thousands of Palestinians and inflicted horrific destruction upon homes and farmland. From this we can conclude that the violence that these Palestinian organizations pursue merely helps Israel to portray itself as defending itself, while serving the interests of the Christian world in its war against Islamic terrorism. In return, Israel expects the US and the West to turn a blind eye to its domination of the occupied territories so that it can perpetuate its ongoing expansion.

At this juncture, it would be interesting to look at the issue of stone-throwing. During the First Intifada, actions challenging the Israeli occupation were primarily nonviolent. These included the determination of opening and closing times for shops, contrary to the orders of the occupation authorities; declarations of independence by Palestinian villages; beginning and ending Daylight Savings Time on different dates than in Israel; boycotts of Israeli consumer goods; demonstrations; the tax strike by residents of Beit Sahour, etc. All of these were nonviolent actions against the occupation. Stone-throwing, also widespread during the First Intifada, enabled Israel to justify its violent response to the Intifada; it has often been stated that a stone can kill. Even so, Israel did not dare to deploy its full military might in response, as it did during the Second Intifada, when acts of terrorism by Palestinians took many Israeli lives.

In the struggle against the separation barrier, too, we are witnessing the same phenomenon. The popular committees in the villages resisting the wall consistently conduct nonviolent actions. Yet nearly every village has its opponents to nonviolence, who claim that the violence of the occupation justifies violence on their own part. They exploit the weekly protest demonstrations and the arrival of Israeli forces to halt them, as an occasion to throw stones at the soldiers. The latter respond by firing teargas canisters, rubber coated bullets, "stink water" cannons and, at times, even live ammunition at the nonviolent demonstrators, not to mention night-time raids to arrest activists. Stone-throwing gives the army the justification to violently quell the struggle. We must remember, of course, that even this is done primarily by employing means generally considered to be non-lethal. By the way, early in the struggle, there were actually incidents where the IDF sent agents provocateurs to participate in Palestinian demonstrations and to throw stones at soldiers, giving the latter grounds to attack the demonstrators.

I believe that only a transition to absolute nonviolence on the part of the Palestinians will undercut Israel's ability to continue exerting violence to maintain the occupation.

Here I must state that, as an Israeli, I have no right to preach to Palestinians how to conduct their struggle against the Israeli occupation. All that I can do is support those Palestinians who have chosen the path of nonviolence and are attempting to persuade their people to join them. I try to interest my fellow Israelis in nonviolence, in the hope that together we may succeed in setting in motion an escalation of nonviolence, culminating in an end to mutual bloodshed and a just peace between our peoples.

PART 5

EXAMPLES OF "DON'T SAY WE DID NOT KNOW"

> *Don't Say We Did Not Know*
>
> The media reported on 19th May, 2008, that IDF soldiers killed a Palestinian youth, who tried to cross the Hawara checkpoint with explosives fixed in water pipes tied to his belt. A female soldier was even decorated...
>
> The boy, Fahmi 'Abed ElJawwad Eldarduk, a ninth grade student, left home with two cellular phones and an earphone. To calm his father he told him he had already passed the Hawara checkpoint before he actually passed it. At about 19:30, after passing the carrousel (rotating gate), the soldiers ordered him to lift his shirt. The cellphone and earphone probably made them suspicious, and they shot him immediately. A Palestinian ambulance arrived after twenty minutes but was not allowed to get near. Only at 23:30 was it allowed to take away the dead body.
>
> IDF soldiers dispersed other Palestinians there, with tear gas and stun grenades. Settlers threw stones, and the soldiers did not stop them.
>
> Whose story should we believe?

The Palestinian village Julud (near the settlements Shvut Rahel and Shilo) has suffered the violence of Israel and its settlers. The village used to have 20,000 dunums of land (dunum = 1000 sq.m); now only some 4000 are left. On 1st January, 2013, in the morning, farmers from the village went with tractors to plough their land. The action had been co-ordinated with the IDF. As they arrived, settlers from the outpost Esh-Kodesh started throwing stones at them. The farmers were forced to beat a retreat. At 1:30 pm, the IDF called them to return, to till their land, but as they arrived they were again attacked by settlers. The soldiers tried to stop the attack. One soldier was injured by settlers, and after a while the army ordered the area to vacated again. The next day, the army permitted the farmers to till the remote half of the area (away from the outpost).

On 3rd January, 2013, at night, settlers began sabotaging cars in the village. A resident heard noise and went out to see what it was. He was injured by attacking settlers. The settlers entered his home and injured his four year old son as well.

On 4th January, 2013, at night, settlers again entered the village and tried unsuccessfully to torch a home.

Soldiers and settlers continue to harass or physically harm Palestinians harvesting their olives.

On Monday and Tuesday, 3rd and 4th November, 2008, soldiers and settlers harassed and attacked a Palestinian family from Kufr Qaddum, who were harvesting their olives near an outpost of the settlement Kedumim. The military had given a permit to them to carry out their harvest.

Some soldiers claimed that the family's tractor was stolen property. The police were called, checked the papers and confirmed that the tractor was the family's property. Settlers threw stones at the family, and a soldier beat the father and hit him over the head with his rifle butt. For nearly an hour soldiers prevented the family from helping their father. Only when more Palestinian farmers arrived were they allowed to help the wounded man. He was taken to hospital and released the next day.

Don't Say We Did Not Know

On Monday, January 20, 2014, the Israeli army ordered residents of the Palestinian Jordan Valley villages of Ibzik (north of Tubas) and Khirbet Yarza (east of Tubas) to evacuate their villages for a while, due to army maneuvers in the area. The villagers refused. The army carried out its maneuvers around them, and they had to remain indoors.

On Wednesday January 22, 2014, the Israeli army demolished two homes in Ibzik and two homes in Khirbet Yarza. It also demolished another 16 livestock pens in both villages.

---- ----

On Monday January 20, 2014, government agents escorted by police arrived and demolished yet again the Bedouin village of Al Arakib in the Negev. The police arrested one of the villagers and released him the next day. Another resident was also arrested the next day.

Don't Say We Did Not Know

Another way to steal land from Palestinians is to declare that land as a *National Park.*

On Monday, 26th January, 2013, before sunrise, staff from the Israel National Parks Authority arrived with Municipality of Jerusalem workmen to Wadi Rababa in Silwan. They were escorted by Border Police, regular police, the dog unit and bulldozers. They broke into privately owned land and started demolishing fences, terraces, sheds and storerooms, and caused damage to ancient olive trees. They undertook work for the creation of a National Park that had been announced in the area.

During the activity they made their dogs attack Palestinians protesting the robbery of their land and damage to their property. Some were injured and some arrested.

Don't Say We Did Not Know

This is what population transfer by "consent" looks like:
On Thursday, 17th January, 2013, IDF soldiers came to the Bedouin village El Maleh in the West Bank's Jordan Valley and demolished 23 homes and 32 animal sheds there. Two hundred people were made homeless.

On Saturday, 19th January, 2013, the army declared the area a closed military zone, and ordered the population to leave until army exercises had finished. After two days the order was removed and the population returned.

On 21st January, 2013, the IDF confiscated the residents' property, including 18 tents donated by the Red Cross following those demolitions.

On 24th January, 2013, the forces returned and demolished two more homes and an animal shed. They proceeded to the village Jiftlik and demolished three homes and two animal sheds.

Don't Say We Did Not Know

The police have escalated its war against the residents of El'Araqib and their supporters.

On Wednesday, 16th February, 2011, government representatives accompanied by police again came to El'Araqib and demolished the village for the 16th time.

The police fired rubber bullets and sponge bullets at the residents. Two were evacuated to hospital. After that, JNF bulldozers continued leveling the ground to prepare it for forestation.

The inhabitants erected their huts again, but the next day they were demolished. People from nearby Rahat who wanted to get to the village cemetery to show solidarity were attacked by police. Some were injured, five detained and one arrested.

Don't Say We Did Not Know

The Israeli government is stepping up its war on Bedouin citizens of the state.

On Thursday, 5th August, 2010, government representatives demolished, yet again, the entire village Twayyel Abu Jarwal.

On Monday, 9th August, 2010, government representatives accompanied by police went to the village Hashem Zane and

177

demolished a house there, making eight people totally home-less, without a roof over their heads.

Then they continued to El-Madbah, where they demolished a house, making four people homeless. In Rakhme, two homes were demolished, making six people homeless. In the village 'Abde, they demolished four tents and a home; 15 were made homeless.

On Tuesday 10th August, 2010 they demolished El'Araqib for the third time. On Tuesday 17th August, 2010, El'Araqib was then demolished for the fourth time!

Don't Say We Did Not Know

On Thursday, 5th August, 2010, IDF forces demolished the en-tire Bedouin village El-Farsiyye in the occupied Jordan Valley, for the second time in two weeks. Twenty six families number-ing some 150 people were made homeless, without a roof over their heads.

---- ----

On Tuesday, 3rd August, 2010, the day before El'Araqib was demolished for the second time, State representatives came to several Bedouin villages in the Negev and demolished homes. In El-Mashash, a home was demolished. Six people were made homeless.

In Qasr Al-Sir, the family (a woman and three children) of a crippled person was forced out, and that person was thrown out of a window, and then the home demolished.

In Jirba, the home of newlyweds was demolished just after the wedding, as well as a shelter used as a *diwan* -- a reception tent for the wedding.

In El-'Shahhbi, a home was demolished making five homeless.

Yesterday, 10th August, 2010, the village of El Araqib was demolished yet again – for the third time in two weeks.

Don't Say We Did Not Know

The IDF and the settlers have been trying to evict the residents of the South Hebron Hills region from their land for years.

One method is by preventing access to their cisterns or any water pumping.

On Saturday, 7th August, 2010, Palestinians from Sussya and Bir el-'Id came to 'Atariyya to pump water from their cisterns. They were accompanied by Israeli human rights activists.

Settlers who arrived from the outpost Mitzpe Yair and the settlement Sussya, started threatening them and tried to empty the water from a tanker that was filled.

Soldiers who were on hand did not try to stop the attack. Instead, they issued a closed military zone order and evicted the Palestinians and their Israeli accompaniers.

Don't Say We Did Not Know

Mahmud 'Ali was born in Dir Dibwan, east of Ramallah, seventy years ago. He married in 1957. In the 1960s, before the Occupation, he went to the USA, where he received citizenship. After some time, he brought his wife and children to the USA.

179

In the 1970s, his wife and children returned to their village, Dir Dibwan. Mahmud then used to visit his family once a year for a month or two. Since his retirement he tried to prolong these visits. The Israeli authorities forced him to go to Jordan every three months and return with a new visa. His wife is seventy years old, is ill and needs his help. About a year ago, the Israelis told him he'd have to wait for a year until he's permitted to return. On January 20, 2007, when he tried to enter the West Bank from Jordan, Israel refused to grant him a visa and his entry was refused.

The village Dir Dibwan is in Area B, which is under Palestinian civil control, but Israel controls entry and exit from it.

Don't Say We Did Not Know

Around noon, 26/02/07, 'Anan El-Tibi climbed his roof, in Nablus, to fix the water system in his house.

His son, Ashraf, a volunteer paramedic, heard that the army was looking for a youngster in a neighboring house.

So he climbed on to the roof to warn his father of possible shooting.

When he reached the roof he was shot in the arm. His father went to help him and then he was shot too. The father was injured in the head and neck. Ashraf tended his father's wounds and called an ambulance. Some soldiers entered the house and one of them identified himself as the shooter. No one in the family was armed or wanted by the army. After a while the soldiers allowed the father to be lowered from the roof to the ambulance; however, they delayed the ambulance for an hour and a half. They bandaged the son. The father died.

Don't Say We Did Not Know

The village Sara is situated west of Nablus, it has 3,000 inhabitants. The school has about 400 pupils. Most of the population makes a living from agriculture.

Between 21 and 28 of November 2006 soldiers have entered the school vicinity. When the pupils went out from the school the soldiers used to throw shock and tear gas grenades, and fired rubber-coated bullets. The inhabitants reported four attacks of pupils in these dates. The villagers approached the International Solidarity Movement (ISM). They arrived to the village on the 28th. As the soldiers arrived with their vehicle the ISM volunteers came near them. The soldiers retreated, with some of the ISM volunteers running after them. Then the soldiers got back again, and backed off when they saw the volunteers, and threw one gas granade.

Since the arrival of the ISM volunteers the attacks on the pupils stopped.

Last month there were several nightly visits by the army that included some breaks into houses.

Don't Say We Did Not Know

The Israeli army has been trying for years now to prevent Palestinians from attending schools in the Qitun neighborhood of Hebron. In 2011, at the beginning of the school year, the army installed a metal-detector at Checkpoint 29, on the way to three schools. Consequently, teachers and pupils held their classes on the roadside, before reaching the checkpoint. Three days later soldiers fired teargas canisters at the school children. Since then, the pupils and teachers pass through the metal-detector.

Soldiers fire teargas and stun grenades at pupils as they walk along the street, at times in response to children's stone-throwing, and at others, with no provocation at all.

On May 5, 2014, soldiers fired two stun grenades at children on their way to school. In response, children threw stones at them. Then the soldiers resorted to firing teargas at the children.

On May 25, 2014, three soldiers ran towards children standing at the entrance to their school house. Some children threw stones at the soldiers, who then fired a stun grenade and two teargas canisters at the children.

On May 27, 2014, as the children were on their way from school, soldiers detained a boy and five teachers for 20 minutes.

Don't Say We Did Not Know

IDF soldiers regularly force Palestinian farmers of the Gaza Strip, ploughing their land near the Israel-Gaza border, to move off it. Not only that, they also then enter the fields and destroy the crops.

On 13th – 14th June 2010, several Beit Hanoun residents were collecting gravel near the border. IDF soldiers opened fire at them and drove them away.

On 15th June 2010, Beit Lahiya farmers went to plough their fields near the border; IDF soldiers shot at them and drove them away.

On 15th - 16th June 2010, farmers from Khan Yunis went

to harvest wheat on their land near the border; IDF soldiers opened fire at them and drove them away.

On 17th June 2010, soldiers again opened fire. This time one of the farmers was hit in the leg.

In all the above cases, the farmers were more than 300 metres from the border.

On 14th June 2010, IDF bulldozers escorted by tanks entered the Gaza Strip to a depth of over half a kilometer and "straightened" the agricultural area.

Don't Say We Did Not Know

The State of Israel continues its war on the Bedouin Talalqa, who live in their village, Twayyel Abu Jarwal. On Tuesday, 18th August, 2009, Twayyel Abu Jarwal was demolished for the 27th time by officials from the Ministry of the Interior, escorted by the police.

In 1952 the state evicted the Talalqa tribe from their own land in Twayyel Abu Jarwal and sent them to what is now the exclusively Jewish town, Meitar. In the 1970s they were transferred to the Bedouin Township Laqiya, which was established at that time. There they were put on land belonging to the Al-Sana' and El-Asad tribes, causing conflicts between the land owners and those transferred to that land.

Due to that conflict, caused by the state, some of the Talalqa had to leave. All their appeals to the state. went unanswered. Having no alternative, some of them returned to their original land, and the state has been trying to evict them from there ever since.

Again, the State has attacked its Bedouin citizens of the Talalqa tribe.

On Sunday, 20th June, 2010, at 4 a.m., police forces barged in to homes of the Talalqa in Laqiya. They broke windows, doors and other property. At the same time, another police force invaded the Talalqa village Twayyel Abu Jarwal. They demolished the entire village (for the 47th time!). At both places 15 youngsters from the village were arrested. Two more villagers were arrested at their work place. At 10 a.m., a police force again entered the Talalqa neighborhood in Laqiya.

The State has been unable to provide the tribe with an alternative living place (which is not on other tribes' lands). This has not prevented the State from wrecking their village over and over again.

---- ----

On Wednesday, 16th June, 2010 State representatives again demolished the village Twayyel Abu Jarwal. They continued onwards, and carried out demolitions in El'Araqib and El-Juruf.

Before day break, on 8th February, 2012, border police units and Golani Brigade soldiers broke into 44 apartments in the Old City of Hebron, and searched them. During the incursion, they smashed the entrance doors. In some homes they broke inner doors and caused further damage. In at least one apartment, it was claimed that they stole money and a boy's watch. In some of the homes the entire families were put in one room during the search. In other cases, families were taken out to the street for some hours.

The whole action took place from 00:30 a.m. and finished at 07:30 a.m.

---- ----

On Monday, 13th February, 2012, government representatives accompanied by police came to the Bedouin village El'Araqib and demolished it.

On Wednesday, 15th February, 2012, government representatives accompanied by police went to a home east of the Bedouin township of Hura and demolished it and then another home, in Hashem Zane (near Nevatim).

Don't Say We Did Not Know

The most recent water bills received by residents of the unrecognized villages, by those with running water, appear to be 69% more expensive than their previous ones.

On Tuesday, 21st February, 2012, government representatives accompanied by police arrived to demolish two homes in Laqia. Three more homes were demolished by their owners, out of fear that they would be charged with the demolition.

On Wednesday, 22nd February, 2012, government representatives accompanied by police came, and using tractors and ploughs, destroyed some 1,500 dunums (dunum=1000 sq.m.) of land sowed with wheat near Bir El-Hamam, Wadi Ruan, and other places. These lands were stolen from the Bedouins by the state, and now the state is offering to lease these lands to

185

the Bedouin for NIS 2 per dunum. By doing so, the Bedouins will be recognizing state ownership over lands that were stolen from them.

Don't Say We Did Not Know

In 1986, the IDF expelled the entire population of the Palestinian village Sussya, following the discovery of an ancient synagogue among the village homes.

After the expulsion, the place was turned into an archeological site. Some who had been expelled returned and settled again on their land. In 2001, the IDF evicted them again. After the second eviction, an appeal to the Supreme Court succeeded, allowing the residents to return under an interim order. In spite of the order, settlers from Sussya and the IDF are attempting to expel the Palestinian residents. Repeated attacks carried out by settlers have caused some of the land to be abandoned. The IDF demolishes residents' homes under the pretext that they were built without permits, which are never given. The IDF has blocked access roads as well.

Now Regavim (a right-wing NGO) and the settlement Sussya are appealing to the Supreme Court for it to order the demolition of the remaining homes in Palestinian Sussya.

On Wednesday, 23rd May, 2012, IDF forces came and demolished a tent used by the people of Sussya as a living area. They also blocked access roads. Four years ago, the family was attacked by settlers and the wife severely wounded.

Don't Say We Did Not Know

Another way of expelling Bedouin from the occupied Jordan Valley is by confiscating their water tanks. Declaration of areas as military zones, home demolitions, expulsions, or taking control of water sources, and so on and so on, are alternative methods of eviction.

On Tuesday, 19th June, 2012, the IDF confiscated three water-tanks near the settlement Bekaot.

On Thursday, 21st June, 2012, the IDF again confiscated two water tanks in El-Milh, south of Bardale.

Don't Say We Did Not Know

For years now, Jewish settlers of the illegal outpost/colony Havat Ma'on (in the South Hebron Hills) have been assaulting elementary school children when these pass by the outpost on their way from their hamlets - Tuba and Mughair Al Abyad - to their schoolhouse in the village of Tawane. In 2004 settlers wounded two international human rights activists who were escorting the children. A public outcry ensued and since then, the Israeli army has supplied escort for the children on their way to and from school. As in many other instances, all along the years the Israeli police in the West Bank manage not to acknowledge the assaults, and certainly not to arrest the assailants.

Often after school the children must wait for a long time until the soldiers arrive to accompany them. A tent has been put up to protect the children while waiting for the soldiers. On March 15 and 16 2013, the Israeli army destroyed this tent.

Yet again, the "Judaea and Samaria" police have confiscated water tankers belonging to Palestinians in the South Hebron Hills region.

On Wednesday, 14th August, 2013 one lorry was confiscated, and on Friday night another one. In total, ten water tankers have been confiscated in recent weeks. In addition, the Civil Administration, IDF and police have demanded that filling water from reservoirs can only take place between 09:00 and 15:00; they have threatened that tankers will be impounded and the filling points closed down. Until now, water operations have been carried out 24 hours a day, to satisfy the demand. The new orders raise concern that tens of thousands of residents will suffer from thirst. Each confiscation entails payment of thousands of shekels in fines, posting of a deposit before trial, as well as payment for removal and storage of the lorry.

At the entrance of Kiryat Arba industrial zone, a tap is operated by settlers selling water to Palestinian carriers at almost three times the normal price. No restrictions there...

---- ----

On Wednesday, 14th August, 2013, government representatives, escorted by police forces, arrived in Bedouin localities in the Negev to demolish homes. In the township of Kseifeh, three homes and a commercial premises were demolished, in Umm Batin a home was destroyed. The following day they demolished two homes in Abu Qrinat, and then they went on to demolish El'Araqib once again.

Don't Say We Did Not Know

Arafat Jaradat of the Palestinian village Se'ir, near Hebron, was arrested on February 18, 2013. He was interrogated by the Shabak (Israel's General Security Services). His death was established on February 23rd 2013. An Israeli coroner declared his death of natural causes. It now appears that an internationally-renowned coroner, Dr. Sebnem Korur Fincanci concluded that he died of torture he suffered under interrogation.

---- ----

On Wednesday, April 2, 2014, government agents escorted by police demolished Bedouin homes in the Negev. A house in the village of A-Zarnouk, north of road 25, was demolished, as was a home in Khirbet Al Watan, south-west of Hura.

On Wednesday, April 9, 2014, again Bedouin homes in the Negev were demolished. Two were destroyed in A-Za'arura, east of Kseife, and one in Abu Krinat, south-west of Aro'er. A home was demolished as well in Umm Batin, east of Tel Sheva. And yet again, Al Araqib was demolished.

Don't Say We Did Not Know

According to the interim agreement between Israel and the PLO, signed after the Oslo Accords, the Gaza fishermen were allowed to fish as far as 20 nautical miles from the shore. After four years, Israel unilaterally restricted the fishing limit to 10 nautical miles. After that the distance was limited again to three nautical miles.

The Israeli Navy continues to attack fishermen from the Gaza

Strip. For example, on 14th February, 2010, naval vessels fired at four fishermen from Beit Lahiya and then detained them. On 16th February, 2010, they fired at and capsized a fishing boat, opposite Beit Lahiya, and then detained the fisherman. On 17th and 18th February 2010, they again shot at fishing boats.

In all the above mentioned cases the fishing boats did not cross the three nautical mile limit.

---- ----

The case of the ownership of the land of the El-Uqbi tribe is being negotiated in the Beer Sheba District Court.

On Sunday, 21st February, 2010, Jewish National Fund employees, accompanied by the Green Patrol, came to the disputed land and started preparing the ground for planting trees; they were accompanied by police who detained Nuri El-Uqbi, ostensibly for interrogation – but really to stop him from struggling against the invasion of the land.

In the evening, the Green Patrol returned to harass Nuri.

Don't Say We Did Not Know

On Sunday, 22nd February, 2009, security forces arrived at the tent of Umm Kamel (of the El-Kurd family) in Sheikh Jarrah neighborhood in East Jerusalem, and demolished it for the fifth time. This follows the expulsion of her family on 9th November, 2008 from the home in which they had lived since 1956 (re. Don't say... # 137).

The state has been using a weak argument to give the property to Jewish settlers, claiming it was owned by Jews before 1948.

At the same time, Umm Kamel has been refused return to

her family's pre-1948 Talbiyyeh home in West Jerusalem.

There is fear of further evictions of Palestinians from the Sheikh Jarrah neighborhood; the Simon the Just (Shimon HaZaddik) settlement is due to expand from a few units to over 200, involving demolition of over 40 homes.

ACKNOWLEDGEMENTS

I first of all owe thanks Sara Carmeli, who has long edited the "Don't Say We Did Not Know" selections. She used this as an opportunity to give me ongoing instruction in the writing of proper Hebrew and constant reminders that the reader does not necessarily know what I do. She continued her editing during periods that were most difficult for her, as well as when she truly did not have time. I thank her from the bottom of my heart

I likewise owe thanks to Adi Shechter, who also edited the selections for a long time, despite all the difficulties she was having. Big thanks to Yishal Seker, who has been editing the selections for long time now and who always volunteered to help whenever there were unexpected problems with the editing. A big thank you, also, to Uri Zackhem, who volunteered to translate this material into English, and to Angela Godfrey-Goldstein, who edited the English. Thanks to Tal Haran, who has been doing this for a long time, now, and was always happy to help out whenever there were unexpected hitches in the English translation process. There were many more friends who came to my aid in times of crisis, but I am not sure I can remember all of them when writing this. My thanks to them.

This entire project would not have been possible without international volunteers, Israeli activists, Palestinian activists and journalists, and sometimes the victims of the abuse themselves. I owe them all a huge thank you!

During my years of writing "Don't Say We Did Not Know," a number of friends encouraged me to write this book. I want especially to mention my friends Moshe Yehudai and Yoav Hess, who repeatedly encouraged me to write it.

My thanks also to several friends who agreed to read the manuscript of the book at different stages, when it wasn't always clear to me whether there was any point in publishing it, and their responses encouraged me.

Thanks to Adam Keller, Gid'on Spiro, Harriet Lewis, Yishal Seker, David Nadel, Ralph Guggenheim, and Raoul Weiss. If I forgot somebody, I hope they will forgive me.

Thanks also to Haya Noah, who went over the section on "The Case of the Bedouins" and made corrections. Thanks to attorneys Khalil al-Amor and Neta Amar, who reviewed, clarified, and corrected the section on "Use of the Legal System." Thanks to Prof. Oren Yiftahel, who helped with some of the statistics I presented.

Throughout the time I was writing this book, I had conversations with many friends about it, and I am sure that some of them gave me useful suggestions, but it is hard for me to recall all of them. Therefore, I will simply thank everyone who was willing to discuss the book and to share their opinions.